Marc Nuttle helped build the conservative movement that brought us Ronald Reagan. In *Moment of Truth* he reminds us that the power lies in our hands to create the kind of America we want to leave for our children and grandchildren.

—TOM A. COBURN, MD
U.S. Senator (R-OK)

Marc Nuttle has been there, done that, and has the T-shirt. He has insight into the political world coupled with his understanding of economics and how the two are intertwined. A must-read for anyone interested in politics or history.

—JACK FARIS
Former President, National Federation
of Independent Business

Agree or argue, but don't ignore. Marc Nuttle's new book is an important contribution to any discussion about the current political landscape.

—ROBERT BENNETT
U.S. Senator (R-UT)

Our children's future is in peril with America at the tipping point. Will we do nothing as America slides into European style Socialism where the government controls and regulates individual rights and opportunities? Marc Nuttle provides the basis for actions to take and the consequences of being a passive observer.

—FRANK MCPHERSON
Chairman and Chief Executive Officer (Retired)
Kerr-McGee Corporation

The economic and government concepts presented in *Moment of Truth* are critical for every American to understand.

—RICHARD J. FOX
Co-Founder, Republican Jewish Coalition and Pennsylvania
Chairman, Ronald Reagan for President 1980

MOMENT *of*
TRUTH

MARC NUTTLE

A STRANG COMPANY

Most STRANG COMMUNICATIONS/CHARISMA HOUSE/SILOAM/FRONTLINE/
EXCEL BOOKS/REALMS products are available at special quantity discounts
for bulk purchase for sales promotions, premiums, fund-raising, and educational needs. For details, write Strang Communications/Charisma House/
Siloam/FrontLine/Excel Books/Realms, 600 Rinehart Road, Lake Mary,
Florida 32746, or telephone (407) 333-0600.

MOMENT OF TRUTH by Marc Nuttle
Published by FrontLine
A Strang Company
600 Rinehart Road
Lake Mary, Florida 32746
www.frontlineissues.com

Unless otherwise noted, all Scripture quotations are from the New King
James Version of the Bible. Copyright © 1979, 1980, 1982 by Thomas Nelson,
Inc., publishers. Used by permission.

Scripture quotations marked KJV are from the King James Version
of the Bible.

Cover Designer: Judith McKittrick
Design Director: Bill Johnson

Library of Congress Cataloging-in-Publication Data:
An application to register this book for cataloging has been submitted to
the Library of Congress.
International Standard Book Number: 978-1-59979-338-2

First Edition

08 09 10 11 12 — 9 8 7 6 5 4 3 2 1
Printed in the United States of America

Dedication

I dedicate this book to the generations.

The past generation:

To my parents and to my mother- and father-in-law, who survived the Depression, defended us in World War II, ran a small business and a family-owned business, and passed on to me a greater opportunity than they inherited.

The present generation:

To my wife, Ann, the example of loving selflessness; my sister, Margy, a committed Christian; my in-laws and extended family who pursue their professions and family-owned businesses.

The next generations:

To my children and their spouses—Marissa, Tommy, Marci, and Blake—who demonstrate passion in their pursuit of law, ministry, and the continued tradition of a family-owned business.

And to my grandchildren—Anna, Tripp, and Jade. May they have the same freedom for self-determination and opportunity that I received from my grandparents.

At what point shall we expect the approach of danger? By what means shall we fortify against it?—Shall we expect some transatlantic military giant, to step the Ocean, and crush us at a blow? Never!—All the armies of Europe, Asia and Africa combined, with all the treasure of the earth (our own excepted) in their military chest; with a Bonaparte for a commander, could not by force, take a drink from the Ohio, or make a track on the Blue Ridge, in a trial of a thousand years.

At what point then is the approach of danger to be expected? I answer, if it ever reach us, it must spring up amongst us. It cannot come from abroad. If destruction be our lot, we must ourselves be its author and finisher. As a nation of freemen, we must live through all time, or die by suicide.

—ABRAHAM LINCOLN
January 27, 1838, Lyceum Address

Contents

Acknowledgments

This book began more than thirty years ago during the Nixon administration when Governor Henry Bellmon's run for the U.S. Senate illustrated to me that the electorate could not only handle change, but also would take control of it. Many people along the way have made contributions, and I am most grateful for the following:

Bill Arnold	Gene Atkinson
Bob Bennett	Father Tom Boyer
Mark Burget	Jeff Butzke
Michael Clifford	Tom Coburn
Don Cogman	Chuck Colson
Wayne Copeland	Mary Fallin
Jack Faris	Dick Fox
Bob Funk	Tommy Garrett
Evelyn Garriss	Burns Hargis
Marion Harrison	Bill Houston
Phil Hurley	Lacy Hunt
Chris Huston	John and Marga Hewko
Frank Hill	Fred Holladay
Jim Inhofe	Barbara Kasoff
Frank Keating	Wes Lane
Gary Lawrence	LaDonna Lee
Eddie Mahe	Tony Marsh
Neal McCaleb	Larry McCarthy
Patrick McGuigan	Rob McLendon
Frank McPherson	Father John Metzinger
Clark Mitchell	Tim Mooney
Janet Moore	Matthew Myers
Rick Neal	Terry Neese
Ian Notley	Paul Ogle

Jim Pappas	Gary Pitchlynn
Ken Privett	Richard Reinhardt
Fritz Rench	Dee Replogle
Steve Rice	Trey Richardson
Joe Rodgers	Lee Rooker
Ed Rollins	Dick Rush
Sal Russo	Dean Schirf
Ken Schuerman	Michael Schwartz
Jim Shearer	Rick Shelby
Don Smith	Marshall Snipes
Renzi Stone	Steve Strang
Lance Tarrance	Kathryn Taylor
Rich Taylor	Chuck Thompson
Bill Tucker	Paul Weyrich
Don Wilber	Don Wood
David Woods	

I am grateful to the staff at Strang Communications, who have been most helpful with the process. They directed me to Jim Nelson Black, who was the editor for this book—and a friend who cares about the content and message of this book. I thank Sam Hammons for his lifelong friendship and personal advice on this book project. Bob Klabzuba and Mike Lynch helped in my interpretation of national and international energy economics and set an example as entrepreneurs.

Dana Murphy provided me with research and, most importantly, prayers. Brent Clark gave his advice unselfishly, and Beverly Allam endured long hours typing the manuscript and offering insightful editorial comments. Special thanks goes to Tracy Campbell for her organizational skills with this project. I have been blessed to work with Tracy for twenty-four years.

Finally I am eternally grateful to my wife and loving partner, Ann, who encouraged me, put up with countless hours of discussion, and patiently helped me organize the themes in this book.

THE CRUCIBLE OF CHANGE

Many people today feel a measure of uncertainty about our nation's future. We may have difficulty expressing it, but many of us feel for the first time in the history of this great country that we may not be able to pass on to the next generation the same opportunities that were passed on to us. We fear that we may be losing control of our destiny and that forces beyond our control are assaulting the culture of freedom we hold dear.

Presidential politics can be unsettling, as candidates of every persuasion battle for attention. They come at us from the Left and the Right, each one claiming to be the answer to America's prayers. They state their claims and smile for the cameras, but still we wonder. Attacks from political opponents can be brutal and humiliating, even in the best of times. We wonder how faithful the various candidates will be to our deeply held beliefs and concerns, so we watch and wait. It's important to be cautious, but this is no time to stand on the sidelines.

Thanks to the wisdom of the Founding Fathers, we the people do have a voice in politics. We can vote, and we can speak to others about our concerns. We can have the confidence of knowing that there are things we can do to protect our children and preserve our nation's godly heritage. Furthermore, we have a God-given mandate to be involved in the choice of our leaders. It's every American's solemn duty, and that is the real message of this book.

The questions we're faced with most often are how to maintain the balance between government programs and individual liberty. Government may very well provide security for the here and now, but sacrificing personal liberty for safety is never a reasonable choice. Thousands of brave Americans, from Bunker Hill to Baghdad, have shed their blood to preserve our heritage of freedom and independence. Their gift to us is the liberty and prosperity we enjoy today. Any suggestion of ignoring that great sacrifice ought to be unthinkable.

Make no mistake; the decisions we make and the leaders we elect in 2008 will determine the future of this nation for a generation. Are we willing to trade our children's future and their freedom for the promises of politicians? Does anyone honestly believe that Washington knows best how we should live our lives? The dividing lines are clear between those on one side who believe the state has all the answers and those on the other who trust the inherent wisdom of the American people. Both sides have persuasive arguments and sophisticated political machinery behind them. The decisions believers make at the polls must be measured against our faith in God and His requirements for living a life of faithfulness and trust in Him. But how will we measure up?

We find ourselves today in a time of transition as great as any in history. The Renaissance, the Industrial Revolution, and the Second World War were all momentous times that changed the world. But today we've come to a time of even greater change, brought about by the rise of China, the development of the Internet, and the emergence of what we now call "nonstate states," meaning political and ideological communities, such as al Qaeda or OPEC, that act with the authority and force of governments. In addition, issues such as climate change and the global AIDS epidemic are changing the political equation. Together, these forces will impact coming generations in ways that will require revolutionary new kinds of problem solving.

We will need great deliberation about the way government works. We will need a new assessment of our national priorities and a new vision for what we want the American culture to become. As we consider all the claims and counterclaims made by pundits and politicians, we will also need sound judgment and godly counsel. As storm clouds continue to gather on the horizon, we often fear that darkness is approaching, and there's no doubt we will face many challenges in the years ahead. We can't avoid it. But with God's help, we can prepare ourselves for what's to come. We can overcome adversity through a renewed commitment to the principles of liberty handed down to us by the founders of our nation.

For help on action steps you can take to make a difference in your future and that of our nation, see networking possibilities discussed on page 202.

A CALL TO FAITHFULNESS

During my career as a Washington lawyer, political consultant, and international adviser, I've witnessed up close and personal the unbelievable hardship placed on families living under Communist rule, and I will relate some of those stories in these pages. Communism claimed to provide all things for all people. All they had to do was give up their freedom, including the freedom to worship a God greater than government. But despite all the rhetoric and unrealistic promises, Communism proved to be the greatest evil ever imposed on mankind.

The performance of Communist regimes is there for the entire world to see, and it is a record of utter and absolute failure. Even in prosperous countries such as China, Communism has had to yield to democratic principles of liberty and free enterprise in order to survive. Yet, the Socialist roots of total government control refuse to die, and the Socialist roots of the European economic system, favored by many on the political Left, pose an even greater threat to America's future.

In the following chapters I will discuss all these things and many other issues the American people need to think about in the coming months. To use our voices and votes effectively, it will help for each of us to have a coherent grasp of these transitional forces and the history that has put them in play. By drawing upon my own thirty-plus-year career in national and international diplomacy, I can offer several real-world examples from the lives of men and women who found themselves in the crucible of change.

I will explore some of the consequences of the choices we're making in this country today. How can we avoid being deceived by false choices? How can we be sure we will be able to determine our children's future as we see fit? What can we do now to improve the situation in this country? And what questions should we be asking in order to balance our security with freedom and faith?

When Ronald Reagan spoke to the nation in what may be his most famous speech, a dozen years before his first presidential campaign, he warned about the dangers of compromising core principles. As a Hollywood actor, Reagan had once supported liberal causes, but when he recognized the emerging signs of liberal influence in the film industry and the risks to our freedom it entailed, he changed his views dramatically and became the standard-bearer for an authentic American conservatism.

In his 1964 speech supporting presidential candidate Barry Goldwater, Mr. Reagan defended the rights of free people to make their own choices. He said, "We are told that the problem is too complex for a simple answer. They are wrong. There is no easy answer, but there is a simple answer. We must have the courage to do what we know is morally right, and this policy of accommodation asks us to accept the greatest possible immorality."[1]

Then governor Reagan began an ideological movement that would set the course of the United States for forty years. His leadership would protect our country as an island of freedom in a sea of Socialism, standing against the Soviet Union and the world forces of big government, big business, and big labor, acting to construct a world-managed economic system.

Compromise and appeasement, he said, are not the answer. As Winston Churchill said in a radio address to the British people during the first year of the Second World War, "The destiny of man is not measured by material computation. When great forces are on the move in the world, we learn we are spirits—not animals." And the great British prime minister added that, "There is something going on in time and space, and beyond time and space, which, whether we like it nor not, spells duty."[2]

Reagan closed his remarks by saying that, "You and I have a rendezvous with destiny. We will preserve for our children this, the last best hope of man on earth, or we will sentence them to take the first step into a thousand years of darkness." Even if we fail, he said, let our children and grandchildren say of us that at least we tried. And let future generations know, beyond any shadow of doubt, that our generation did all we could do.[3]

It is my hope that this book may awaken the same sort of passion in your heart and that the principles discussed in these pages may provide you with new resources and a new resolve to stand defiantly against the forces of darkness. The decisions you will be asked to make over the coming year will demand wisdom, deliberation, and godly counsel. It will mean thinking clearly about the alternatives and speaking with conviction to your friends and associates. But as you do, you can be confident in the knowledge, as Paul says in Philippians 1:6, that He who has begun a good work in you will be faithful to complete it.

That may be the best encouragement of all.

Chapter 1

FOR SUCH A TIME AS THIS

There is a tide in the affairs of men,
Which, taken at the flood, leads on to fortune.[1]
— WILLIAM SHAKESPEARE

There's a growing sense of anxiety among many Americans today. We feel we're losing control of our destiny. Many large corporations seem to be motivated by greed with little or no consideration for traditional ethical standards. Labor organizations are more concerned with controlling their members than actual productivity. Health organizations appear more concerned with making money than saving lives. And our biggest concern is that the foundational institutions of our democracy no longer seem to be acting for the greater good of the American people.

In the aftermath of the 2006 midterm elections, the approval rating of Congress fell to an all-time low of just 11 percent.[2] This means that 89 percent of the American public believes that Congress is not doing its job. Furthermore, 74 percent of the public believe that the nation is on the wrong track.[3]

There's a sense that state legislators and local government officials are more interested in their own aggrandizement than their mission to serve the public's interests. When the public becomes this doubtful and suspicious of the core institutions of their society, it's only natural that they should lose hope and become fearful for the future.

At the same time, pressures are mounting around the world, casting an ominous shadow over the American psyche. What are we to think of the rise of China and increased competition for jobs and manufacturing? What's going on with the sudden emergence of India and the new challenges in software production and intellectual property rights? And what about the impact of the Internet on all aspects of business and culture? In addition, we're concerned about the ongoing threat of terrorism here and abroad, and the rise of the nonstate state, all of which seem to threaten our ability to control our own destiny.

There is a growing concern among many people that they will not be able to pass on to their children a better world than the one they received from their parents and grandparents. The desire to make life better for the next generation is an admirable trait. But too often we feel as if there's nothing we can do to make things better. The economy is undergoing such rapid and unpredictable change that many people have doubts about their future prosperity. Anxiety over illegal immigration and other pressures from abroad is growing daily. Recession appears imminent, and fuel prices have not come down.

We can see that our culture is under attack by many powerful forces from within and without our own borders. With the overwhelming flood of goods from China and other places, we're no longer certain the United States can continue as the leading economic power in the world. Third-world countries are taking manufacturing jobs away from American workers, often with an unfair advantage. In fact, we're no longer confident that there will even be good jobs for our children when their time comes.

BUILDING A BETTER TOMORROW

The new buzzword among many in government circles and the mass media today is *globalization*. But we have to wonder, why are so many people talking about global issues when we have so many problems here at home? A lot of people have lost faith in the government's ability to act intelligently and solve America's problems, so what makes them think they'll do any better with problems on a global scale?

There seems to be no accountability and no one to whom we can present our petitions for redress. We may as well be back in 1775, when a distant power, such as England's King George, in the words of the Declaration of Independence, exhibited always "a history of repeated injuries and usurpations, all having in direct object the establishment of an absolute tyranny..."[4] Institutions that are supposed to act in the best interest of all Americans now seem to be acting on behalf of the few. Legal rulings that defy all the traditional standards of right and wrong are handed down routinely by the federal courts, while federal and state legislatures are busily passing half-baked new laws without any evidence of common sense, compassion, or answerability to the people.

We've faced tough times before, of course. In 1974, an unpopular president, Richard Nixon, resigned his presidency to save the nation the trauma of an impeachment trial. Through all the stresses of that troubled year, the public felt the same depths of anxiety we feel today. We had just experienced an unpopular war in Vietnam and were in the aftermath, dealing with deep, emotional, national wounds. Economic conservatives felt betrayed because of executed price controls, and the public felt it had been lied to and misled as a result of the Watergate cover-up.

But right in the middle of all that turmoil, something remarkable happened. Conservatives began working together at the grassroots level, city by city and state by state. By 1975 they were taking matters into their own hands, building new organizations and working together for change. They defined who they were and made no apologies for it. As a result, they became one of the most formidable political movements in modern history.

Part of that new movement was the Christian Right, but they weren't identified that way when they first began. The Christian political movement began with groups of individuals who, state by state and district by district, took a close look at their core values and principles and then recommitted themselves to defending those values at the polls. They weren't concerned about what the rest of the country thought. They defined themselves first and then projected their principles to the public at large. They let their standards be known, and little by little over time they took a leadership role in restoring confidence in the culture and the American way of life.

Today, in the middle of another election year, we find ourselves at a similar moment of truth.

Several of the candidates for the nation's top job have certain attributes that are attractive. And, of course, each candidate has certain negative traits that raise questions and concerns. Part of the anxiety for conservative voters is the fact that there's no one in the race comparable to "the great communicator," Ronald Reagan, whose vision for America was so clear and so optimistic. We were comfortable with Reagan's "big-tent" approach, but we haven't found anyone to take his place.

In reality, the Reagan coalition had many diverse elements. Some parts of the coalition were never comfortable with the other parts under that big tent. What President Reagan provided, however, was the confidence to walk into the tent, to take a stand with others with whom we had little natural affinity, and yet, not to feel threatened by being in partnership with them. We knew that the values Ronald Reagan represented were trustworthy and consistent, and that gave us our sense of unity. The beliefs Reagan expressed so confidently in his speeches and other public appearances didn't change with the times, the seasons, or the circumstances. We had confidence in the premise he set forth that our core values are eternal and nonnegotiable.

When we walked out of that tent, we still maintained our individual identity as we defined it. For example, a business executive who was secular in his religious beliefs could stand in the same tent with an evangelical Christian on the religious Right. For one person the concern might be taxes or the economy or the high cost of social programs; for the other it would be the sanctity of human life or the chaos in the public schools. But each could go back to his or her community and speak confidently to his or her peers about the issues the party supported.

The cooperative atmosphere of that tent seems to have been lost in recent years, and that conservative coalition needs to be reestablished. In these troubled times, we need friends who agree with us in principle. However, the process begins with individuals who know their own mind, who have the confidence to define their core values, and who are secure in what that definition represents.

TOWARD A BETTER ECONOMY

In the speech that would define American conservatism for years to come, called "A Time for Choosing," Ronald Reagan set the standard by which decisions regarding our nation's future and the safety of our children must be made. He said the Founding Fathers understood that "government can't control the economy without controlling people." And they also knew that whenever a government sets out to control the citizens, it eventually uses "force and coercion to achieve its purpose."

The point of those stirring words, as Mr. Reagan explained, was that we have come to a time for choosing. Either we accept responsibility for our own lives and day-to-day choices, or we give up on the hope of the American Dream. There are people in the media, the think tanks, and government offices who would love nothing better than to tell us how to live our lives, but that's not the American ideal. Reagan warned that the hour is already late, and he said:

> Government has laid its hand on health, housing, farming, industry, commerce, education, and, to an ever-increasing degree, interferes with the people's right to know. Government tends to grow; government programs take on weight and momentum, as public servants say, always with the best of intentions, "What greater service we could render if only we had a little more money and a little more power." But the truth is that outside of its legitimate function, government does nothing as well or as economically as the private sector of the economy.[5]

When a government controls the people it purports to represent, loss of freedom and personal liberty is the inevitable consequence. Without freedom, there is no opportunity. And without opportunity our children will have no future. Mr. Reagan also said in that speech that, "If some among you fear taking a stand because you are afraid of reprisals from customers, clients, or even government, recognize that you are just feeding the crocodile hoping he'll eat you last." As Winston Churchill had warned at the height of the Second World War, appeasement merely delays the inevitable. It never leads to peace but to surrender. The only way for freedom-loving people to deal with tyrants is to stand up defiantly and defeat them.

When Reagan delivered that famous stump speech on behalf of Barry Goldwater, the choices this nation faced were primarily focused within our own borders. Since the end of the Second World War, we had become the world's leading manufacturer and the greatest commercial engine the world had ever seen. Europe still influenced American policy makers, but the European model was uniquely different from our own. Europe's economy was based on a system of managed growth: that is, big business, big government, and big labor working in concert to manage the resources of those nations for the benefit of the people. It was state Socialism of a kind that America had scrupulously avoided ever since the founding era.

Essentially, there are two very different models of government. The European model calls for more government, more centralized control, and a managed economy. The American model, on the other hand, calls for free enterprise, less control, and a market-based economy. In an atmosphere of open and free competition, the best products and services will prosper while those that fail to satisfy the customer will ultimately disappear. Ronald Reagan saw this distinction between a controlled economy and a market-based economy as a critical concern for America's future. And he was right. He called Europe's model of managed government and less freedom a form of "darkness," and he pledged to protect America's children from a thousand years of darkness by refusing to take even a single step toward the Socialist alternative.

As the United States faces more economic competition from China, the debate rages about what form of government is best suited to protect jobs and provide for our economic growth. Liberals again are calling for the European model of more government intervention in the marketplace. They claim that such a managed economic system, like the ones historically established in Europe, will render the best results for economic prosperity in a global economy. But does the evidence support this proposition?

Since 1980, Germany has declined in its share of world economic capacity, Gross Domestic Product (GDP), from 7 percent to less than 5.5 percent. China has increased its share of world GDP from 1 percent to over 5.5 percent in the same period of time. Germany is one of the leading European economies. The European example has not kept pace with China.

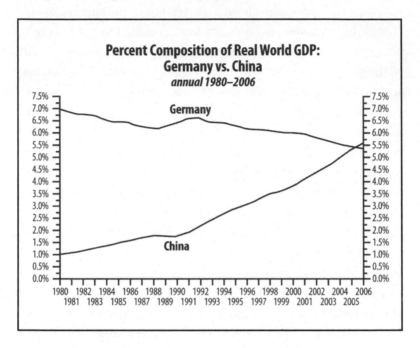

The cry from liberals, then as now, was that capitalism is an outmoded economic system. Only a welfare state, they argued, could effectively distribute goods through a planned economy. It was a dangerous philosophy then and remains so to this day. But that was the mainstream debate until Reagan was elected as America's fortieth president in 1980.

I was a young fieldman for the conservative movement during the 1978 and 1980 elections. I served on President Reagan's Presidential Transition Team in 1980, and I was then chosen as one of his campaign field counsels in the 1984 elections. I remember vividly the calls coming into our transition headquarters from government officials in Europe asking us, "How did you change the debate successfully from 'how to implement a welfare state' to 'a welfare state versus a free-enterprise capitalistic system'?"

The idea that free enterprise and free markets provided the best model for a nation's economy was gaining momentum around the world, thanks in large measure to Reagan's strong stand. Day by day and step by step, his administration successfully pushed through tax cuts to support the principle of supply-side economics. Congress passed laws that recognized that free enterprise has a major role to play in public policy. Meanwhile, the president insisted that free people should be able to make decisions for themselves and their families, based not on what the state allows but on what they wish to do within the natural constraints of the law. And that philosophy allowed the marketplace model in this country to become the greatest engine of economic prosperity the world has ever known.

STORM CLOUDS OF CONTROVERSY

Despite America's record of more than thirty years of unprecedented prosperity and success in business and industry, there are still many people in positions of authority in this country who would like to turn back the clock and go back to the European model of a controlled economy. Make no mistake; how we respond to this challenge will have a tremendous impact on the nation for years to come and will dramatically impact our children's future. We will be called upon to make some tough choices, but if the Socialist model prevails, we will be in for a time of darkness and disappointment like nothing we've ever seen.

Unfortunately, some of this country's best-known legislators, economists, and academics refuse to give up on the Socialist model. Even though the entire world witnessed the collapse of state Socialism in Russia and Eastern Europe during the 1990s, some of these self-appointed "experts" still believe that centralized control and limits on individual freedom are the best guarantees of a secure future for all. We ought to be very suspicious of this kind of thinking.

In the early 1980s, I served as legal counsel to a group called the National Tax-Limitation Committee (NTLC). That organization worked for a federal constitutional amendment for a balanced budget. Its chairman, Lewis K. Uhler, was a Reagan cabinet official from the president's home state of California. The distinguished economist Milton Friedman was a board adviser of the NTLC, and I was fortunate enough to be serving as staff counsel for the organization when Dr. Friedman testified before the Senate Judiciary Committee about the balanced-budget constitutional amendment.

The issue was being hotly debated at that time, and the hearing became a free-for-all on the relative merits of free enterprise and state Socialism. Despite being outnumbered by a long list of liberal senators who argued vehemently for the Socialist model, Dr. Friedman easily won the day. Ted Kennedy, a well-known senator on the committee, argued forcefully that Socialism was a better and fairer distributor of goods and services to the people. And he claimed that a balanced-budget constitutional amendment would curtail the government's cash flow.

I'll never forget Dr. Friedman's reply. "Senator," he said, "Socialism hasn't worked in six thousand years of recorded history. Why won't you give up on it?" Then, to everyone's chagrin, the senator rose imperiously to his feet and glared down from the bench and replied, "It hasn't worked in six thousand years of recorded history because it didn't have *me* to run it." I can tell you, no one bought that line, but it took the brilliant articulation of Milton Friedman and the courageous leadership of Ronald Reagan to make the liberals face reality.[6]

President Reagan had fought the Socialist influence in California for many years and even waged a one-man campaign for years to stop Communist agitators from taking over the Screen Actors Guild. He had firsthand experience on that battlefront and never wavered from his position of strength. Some of his ardent resolve is captured in that 1964 speech at the Republican National Convention in San Francisco.

He wanted the nation to understand that it's time for all Americans to ask ourselves if we still understand and appreciate the freedoms won for us by our Founding Fathers. President James Madison said, "We base all our experiments on the capacity of mankind for self-government." The idea enshrined in the Constitution that government is responsible to the people, and not the other way around, Reagan said, is still the most unique idea in all the annals of human history. The founders of our nation declared that in a free nation the people are and ought to be sovereign and the state is duty-bound to serve the interests of the electorate.

TIME FOR CHOOSING

For almost two centuries, Reagan said, this nation has proven that free men, rightly informed, have the capacity for self-government. Unfortunately, there are people who tell us continually that we must choose between Left and Right or, as has been suggested more recently by liberal strategists, there needs to be a "third way," which they call the "safe middle ground." But Reagan wasn't persuaded. He said in his speech, "I suggest to you there is no left or right, only an up or down. Up to the maximum of individual freedom consistent with law and order, or down to the ant heap of totalitarianism; and regardless of their humanitarian purpose those who would sacrifice freedom for security have, whether they know it or not, chosen this downward path."

As the Roman philosopher and historian Plutarch once warned, "The real destroyer of the liberties of the people is he who spreads among them bounties, donations, and benefits."[7] But this is precisely what the Socialist model demands—a welfare system that weakens individual initiative by taking from the most productive and giving to others as the state sees fit. Reagan said there were some people in government and the media who couldn't see a fat man standing beside a thin man without assuming the fat man got that way by taking advantage of the thin one. The reality of personal responsibility and personal weakness never entered their minds. So the answer to all the problems of society was to call for more and bigger government.

Television commentator Howard K. Smith even said in one of his editorials, "The profit motive is outmoded. It must be replaced by the incentives of the welfare state." And he argued, "The distribution of goods must be effected by a planned economy."[8] Another defender of the welfare-state model defined liberalism as a system for meeting the material needs of the masses through the full power of centralized government. But again, Reagan was having none of it. He said in his speech, "I for one find it disturbing when a representative refers to the free men and women of this country as *the masses*; but beyond this, the full power of centralized government was the very thing the Founding Fathers sought to minimize."

The founders of our nation knew that government couldn't control the economy without first controlling the people. But is that what the American people wanted: a government that controls their every move and determines when, where, and how they can live their lives? Mr. Reagan put the burden of choice where it belonged—not with government but with the people themselves. "Either we accept the responsibility for our own destiny," he said, "or we abandon the American Revolution and confess that an intellectual belief in a far-distant capitol can plan our lives for us better than we can plan them ourselves."

The movement that Ronald Reagan started in the early 1960s transformed our country. But forty years later the conservative base is divided, and not just divided by issues. The issues and concerns are the same. Rather, we're divided over who to follow and which direction to go. It's vital that we understand that participation is not optional. We have to be involved, and we have to make the hard choices. Not participating means that we're willing to delegate our children's future to the unknown.

Doing nothing is like leaving your child with a stranger. It may work out fine, but why would you risk it? If you don't participate in the electoral process, and if you don't vote, people who are dedicated to a philosophy very different from your own may very well overwhelm you. In my opinion, it's a betrayal of our ancestors who sacrificed so greatly for our freedom not to be involved in choosing our leaders and the policies they're obliged to support.

THE MAKING OF A LEADER

It's important to remember that Ronald Reagan didn't come into his own as a political candidate until the spring of 1980. He lost the Republican Party nomination for president in 1976 to Gerald Ford. Gerald Ford lost in a close election to Jimmy Carter. When Ronald Reagan again sought the Republican nomination in 1980, several candidates entered the race with the mistaken impression that Reagan couldn't possibly win the nomination. In fact, Reagan didn't become a dominant factor in the presidential race until he showed his fortitude in a now-famous encounter during the New Hampshire debates.

The best retelling of what happened that night comes from Reagan himself in his autobiography, *An American Life*. By the winter of 1980, he says, everybody except the other five or six Republican candidates felt that the primary had come down to a contest between himself and George Bush. The Iowa caucuses were finished, and Bush had won. Later, when both Reagan and Bush were on the trail in New Hampshire, the publisher of the *Nashua Telegraph* offered to sponsor a debate between the two of them on the Saturday evening preceding the primary, and both accepted.

"Understandably," says Reagan, "this brought howls from the other candidates." When Senator Bob Dole complained to the Federal Election Commission about the way the event was being handled, the Reagan campaign offered to pay the full cost of the debate, and the editors accepted. However, the newspaper was still determined to question only two candidates, Reagan and Bush, and refused to provide chairs for the five others who were standing there looking embarrassed. So Reagan explained:

> Unable to understand what was going on, the audience hooted and hollered and urged us to proceed. I decided I should explain to the crowd what the delay was all about and started to speak. As I did, an editor of the Nashua newspaper shouted to the sound man, "*Turn Mr. Reagan's microphone off.*"
>
> Well, I didn't like that—we were paying the freight for the debate and he was acting as if his newspaper was still sponsoring it. I turned to him, with the microphone still on, and said the first thing that came to my mind: "*I am paying for this microphone, Mr. Breen.*" Well, for some reason my words hit the audience, whose emotions were already worked up, like a sledgehammer. The crowd roared and just went wild. I may have won the debate, the primary—and the nomination—right there.[9]

From that day forward, people knew that Reagan was a man of principle. He had the courage of his convictions, and it showed. He wouldn't become the true front-runner until after the South Carolina primary, two months later, but after New Hampshire it was clear that he was the most dynamic candidate in the race.

The process of picking a leader is difficult, but it's an important one. It starts with each individual voter knowing what they believe in and what they are truly committed to for the long term. If the voters know what they want and continue to stand by their convictions, a leader who adheres to those values will emerge. This is one of the great lessons of the American democracy. Strong principles demand strong leaders, but when the people make it clear that they will settle for nothing less, strong leaders will come forth. We must always maintain our commitment to that view and offer it as a lighthouse for the world.

THE ONGOING CHALLENGE

As Ronald Reagan saw the clouds of darkness looming on the horizon in that earlier time, we find ourselves today facing problems of even greater consequence on a global scale. Many of our problems were never envisioned by the men and women of that era, but the choices are the same. The debate is as old as the ages. Do we want government to provide for our every need, from cradle to grave? Should government be our master and provider, or is government's role merely to facilitate our own individual initiative, allowing each of us to use our God-given talents and skills as we see fit?

These are the only options. Either we sacrifice freedom for security—which is one of the historic risks of all great societies in times of transition—or we make a renewed commitment to limit the interference of government in our lives so that each person can achieve prosperity in their own way for themselves and their families. Capitalism means free enterprise. It involves risk and failure, but it also allows second and third chances and the opportunity to make new arrangements on our own terms. Socialism, on the other hand, means the loss of freedom for the sake of security at all costs.

Now, I know there are some who would say that this is an unfair characterization. But I submit that it is not only correct but also the essential difference between the two dominant forms of government competing on the world stage today. Government control over every aspect of daily life is the price societies must pay for the promise of cradle-to-grave security, whereas the freedom to achieve your own success and follow your own ideals—within the reasonable constraints of the law—naturally involves a certain amount of risk. But is it worth the risk? Benjamin Franklin certainly thought so when he said, "Those who would give up essential liberty to purchase a little temporary safety deserve neither liberty nor safety."[10] And I believe he was right about that.

The managed government approach is what we see in much of the world today, and it is no accident that the United States enjoys such a large share of the world's wealth, prosperity, and freedom of opportunity. There are signs of dissent in Europe today as countries such as France and Great Britain are beginning to question some of their earlier assumptions about free markets and controlled economies.

Even Communist China and other third-world countries are beginning to emulate certain aspects of the American model. Nevertheless, the European model is state Socialism, however you define it. In general, this is what the term *Europeanization* means today. Unfortunately, there are people in Washington who would have us believe that the European model is the right way for this country as well.

In most countries, people still have to get permission from the government before they can launch a new business or engage in any sort of entrepreneurial activity. The European Union talks about entrepreneurship as a priority, yet they fail to embrace even the simplest principle of free enterprise—that if it's not illegal, you can do it. Corporations such as FedEx, Apple, and Microsoft would never have gotten permission from the government to start those businesses if they had to abide by European standards. No bureaucrat would have been able to foresee the outcome of those ventures at the start, and any attempt to experiment with new methods would have been regulated and taxed to death.

For most of our history, the American people understood the importance of personal and economic freedom very well. It was a uniquely American concept that developed naturally as a consequence of the American Revolution and what Abraham Lincoln called "a new birth of freedom." Following the Watergate fiasco of the mid-seventies; however, the electorate was profoundly disappointed and frustrated with Washington. No national figure was talking about the importance of economic freedom in those days, and it was only when Ronald Reagan began to speak out about the dangers of Socialism and managed economies during the 1976 and 1980 presidential campaigns that these issues became matters of concern for the general public.

A NEW UNITY OF PURPOSE

Many people had lost faith in our government at that time, and in the 1976 elections the nation made a sudden lurch to the Left by electing a Southern Democrat who identified himself as a "born-again Christian." Jimmy Carter had been a naval officer and governor of a Southern state and seemed to be uncorrupted by political ambition. No one knew much about him, and many voters were willing to take a risk Consequently, the election went to Carter. Republicans had lost forty-three seats in the House of Representatives in 1974. Carter's victory appeared to give the Democratic Party a lock on government for years to come. Ronald Reagan proved by his election in 1980 that the Conservative movement was on the rise, looking for a leader.

During this same time, the liberal media had enflamed public opinion by warning that Ronald Reagan was a right-wing fanatic who would lead the country into a nuclear confrontation with the Soviets. And further, they opined that his concept that less government would actually make us more prosperous, more secure, and more independent from the rest of the world was not only naïve but also ridiculous.

The future of the Republican Party looked bleak for a time, but it only took four years of the Carter presidency for the American people to realize they had made a big mistake. The nation was in desperate need of hope, but President Carter was saying that our best days were all in the past and we needed to scale back our standard of living. The Soviet Union was an imposing adversary, and the specter of nuclear holocaust was ever present. Voters were looking for a new sense of optimism about the future of their country, and in 1980 the nation turned a corner to a period that would become known as "Morning in America."

In the months following the 1976 elections, three new conservative alliances merged into what would become the most successful grassroots movement in history. Four years later, that force would begin to impact national politics as nothing had ever done before. They were the New Right, the Christian Right, and the economic supply-side Right. These groups didn't come together overnight, and there were moments of uncertainty along the way, but the process began at that time with a new unity of purpose that brought these disparate interests together.

They emerged, state by state, uncoordinated and with little knowledge of each other in the beginning. Individual members became active politically because they believed that the American culture was in danger. They weren't unduly concerned about their own personal risk—the cost didn't matter, because they felt their way of life was being threatened. And no cost would have been too great to pay to preserve the culture.

One such person was Don Nickles. He managed a small family-owned machine tooling business in Ponca City, Oklahoma, Nickles Machine. In 1978, Don came to the conclusion that the future of his family-owned business was threatened by the destructive programs of big government. He decided to do something about it. Without any network, or state or national backing, he ran for the state senate. It wasn't an easy decision for him. Ponca City is two hours from the Oklahoma state capitol. The commute would be hard on his business and on his family. But Don had decided that it was that important. The ability of his family-owned business to survive was at stake, let alone the hope of pursuing prosperity. He had realized the classic proposition: If not me, who? If not now, when? His hope for not only his children's future but also the future of all children necessitated action now.

Don won that state senate seat at the ripe old age of twenty-nine. Two years later he called me and informed me that he intended to run for the Senate. I said, "Don, you're *in* the Senate." He replied, "No, I mean the United States Senate."

Needless to say, I was surprised. I had supported him for the state senate. He had great talent and potential. Yet one usually gets a little more experience before running for statewide office. But as I listened to him and thought about the possibilities, I became convinced. Don saw before anyone else that a national movement was jelling around a new conservative agenda, a call started by Ronald Reagan in 1964. Don felt that to make a significant difference, he had to get to the national level. He ran as a small family-owned business owner. People related to his message of less government and to him personally as a family man. Don won the U.S. Senate seat in 1980 by the largest margin for a Republican in state history at that time. All over the country, other individuals got involved the same way, not knowing how they were going to do it but confident that something had to be done. Republicans captured the Senate, an outcome that no one predicted earlier in the year. The grass roots led themselves and changed history.

When Don won, he was too young to take office. He turned thirty-two before he was sworn into office. Don served exceptionally, providing leadership and sound judgment on business and moral issues. He served twenty-four years without a hint of scandal or controversy. In all fairness, his wife, Linda, gave meaning to the term "the better half." An elegant, reserved, articulate woman, Linda was a leader and role model in her own right. As a combination, they are above comparison. It is now time for other small-business owners to step up and take the Reagan vision forward for another forty years. It simply requires taking a stand, addressing the issues, and providing leadership.

REBUILDING THE BASE

I began my own career with the New Right at the national level in the mid-seventies. After all the upheavals of the sixties and the chaos of the Nixon years, I felt compelled to get involved somewhere and work for responsible change. So I went to Washington and joined the staff of an organization called the Committee for the Survival of a Free Congress (CSFC), which was headed by Paul Weyrich. The name of that nonprofit group has since been shortened to the Free Congress Foundation, but in those years I worked as an analyst and consultant for congressional campaigns all over the country, helping to put qualified conservatives in Congress.

As I made my way around the country, I began seeing conservatives of many stripes who were coming together independently, on their own volition, united around the general principles and themes of conservatism. It was obvious that the grass roots were reconstituting themselves without any recognizable national leadership, building new coalitions around these three basic movements. We didn't know enough in 1976 to make much of it; however, by 1978 we were beginning to see where this could lead. The nucleus of a new consensus of conservative voters was coming together, almost invisible to the outside world.

In trying to determine what was driving the new Christian Right movement, I decided I needed to fly out to California on my own dime to meet with some of the activist pastors in that part of the country. I wanted to understand their issues, and I also wanted to find out the extent and depth of their networks. On one of those visits, I was just coming out of a leading pastor's study when I met Eddie Mahe, who was just coming in. At that time, Eddie was the executive director of the Republican National Committee (RNC). He told me he was there doing exactly the same thing I was—trying to find out what was going on with the evangelicals. As far as I know, that was the first ever meeting between the New Right, the Christian Right, and the national Republican Party.

In 1978 we began seeing this new consensus at work, making political gains in several key states. Conservatives hadn't switched parties in 1976. They simply hadn't voted. In 1976 conservatives were disappointed in Richard Nixon and refused to vote for Gerald Ford after he pardoned Nixon. Consequently, large numbers of conservatives decided to take a chance on Jimmy Carter, and that's what turned the tide for the Democrats in the 1976 election. But now, with the growing interest in Ronald Reagan as a candidate in the 1980 election, the grass roots began getting involved once again. The stump speech Reagan gave in support of Barry Goldwater back in 1964 had started it, and now the image of a credible, charismatic, principled leader was beginning to bear fruit in the form of a large and dynamic political base.

Even though many national leaders were still in denial about the public's demand for greater economic and personal freedom, grassroots activists weren't discouraged in the least. They wanted their issues to be addressed, and they found companions with similar views and expectations to join the cause. As Milton Friedman expressed it, the ducks aligned on their own into a *v*, just waiting for the right leader. Eventually, Ronald Reagan took his position as the leader of that movement, having come in with the supply-siders.

A New Consensus

Thanks to the undeniable failures of the Carter administration in dealing with the economy and foreign affairs—including especially the Iran Hostage Crisis—the American people saw Reagan's optimistic outlook as a breath of fresh air, and they elected the Republican candidate in a landslide. Promising to reduce federal spending, cut taxes, and strengthen our national defense, President Reagan and Vice President George Bush claimed 51 percent of the popular vote and 489 votes in the Electoral College. In addition, Republicans gained 12 more seats in the Senate, giving them control of that body for the first time since 1954. Equally important, the conservative movement was thriving all across America, primarily on the basis of Reagan's conservative values and winsome personality.

Because of the choices made by grassroots activists after the Nixon resignation in 1974, Ronald Reagan was able to restore the confidence of the nation and lead the country and the entire free world through one of the greatest transitions in history. In 1984 Reagan won reelection in a landslide surpassed only by George Washington, who ran unopposed. The collapse of the Soviet Union and the dramatic end of the cold war in 1989–1990 may go down in history as the greatest legacy of the Reagan years.

Unfortunately, the Reagan era ended after eight years, and during the Bush era, which came afterward, Congress returned to the old economic agenda. Today, two decades later, the United States government seems to be drifting once again toward the bigger and more intrusive government of the European model. The European Union has been formed, the European economic community has been established, and there is now a common currency and talk of a new United States of Europe. Some of the leading academics and public intellectuals in this country are back to their old habits, suggesting that America should walk in lockstep with Europe into a North Atlantic–managed growth system. The hotly debated North American Free Trade Agreement (NAFTA) is a big part of that debate.

So, the crises the grass roots faced in 1975, we face again today. Managed government and the threat of Europeanization are being proposed once again by political leaders on the Left as a viable solution for our economic woes. We're engaged in a troublesome and never-ending war in the Middle East that is being exploited by political interests and opportunists of all stripes for their own advantage. At the same time, fiscal conservatives are angry about the large federal deficits, out-of-control entitlement programs, and the ongoing shake-up in the real estate and investment markets.

But once again, America's crisis of confidence is producing a new demand for change, and, as Milton Friedman pointed out, this is the environment in which true progress can begin. In his book *Capitalism and Freedom*, Friedman writes that, "Only a crisis—actual or perceived—produces real change. When that crisis occurs, the actions that are taken depend on the ideas that are lying around. That, I believe, is our basic function: to develop alternatives to existing policies, to keep them alive and available until the politically impossible becomes the politically inevitable."[11]

Once again conservatives are reconstituting themselves into new organizations and alliances. And once again the ducks are forming into a *v*, looking for the leader who will emerge to take us in the right direction. However, because of all the turmoil this nation has endured over the past three decades, we're able to see things today in ways we could never have seen them in 1976 or 1980. Trusting others to do for us what we must do for ourselves is no longer an option. And staying home, as conservative voters did in 1974 (and again, I might add, in 2006), is a recipe for disaster.

What Ronald Reagan began in 1964 peaked as an ideological movement in 2004 with the reelection of George W. Bush. This marks a forty-year cycle of fundamental change and growth toward freedom. Before President Reagan took office in 1981, the only establishment debate recognized by the mainstream leaders or national journalists centered on the details of how to structure a managed economy. No argument of less government was ever entertained. Big government versus small government became the debate after 1980. Because of world forces in motion and the high disapproval rating the public has of government in general, the people are anxious about what the future holds. The Reagan vision must now be embraced in a new cycle or it will be lost for generations.

What is needed now is a new sense of resolve and a new commitment to make our views and values known, to come together in a new consensus with those who share our views, and to work hard for the victory we desire. To leave the process to chance would be unthinkable. Who knows but what, as Scripture says, we have come here for such a time as this?

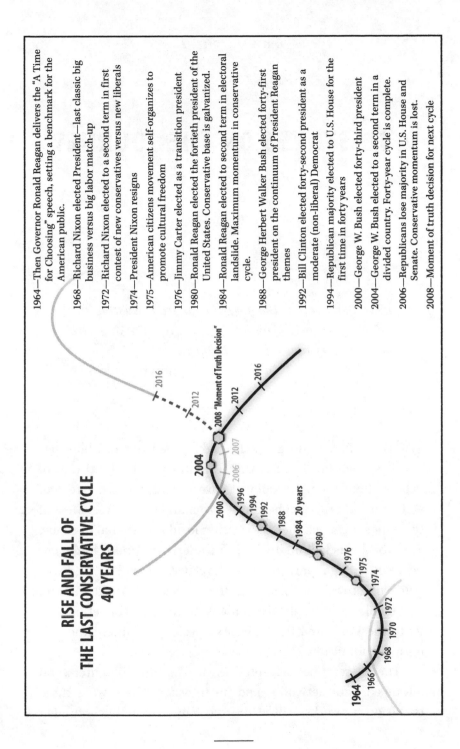

RISE AND FALL OF
THE LAST CONSERVATIVE CYCLE
40 YEARS

1964—Then Governor Ronald Reagan delivers the "A Time for Choosing" speech, setting a benchmark for the American public.

1968—Richard Nixon elected President—last classic big business versus big labor match-up

1972—Richard Nixon elected to a second term in first contest of new conservatives versus new liberals

1974—President Nixon resigns

1975—American citizens movement self-organizes to promote cultural freedom

1976—Jimmy Carter elected as a transition president

1980—Ronald Reagan elected the fortieth president of the United States. Conservative base is galvanized.

1984—Ronald Reagan elected to second term in electoral landslide. Maximum momentum in conservative cycle.

1988—George Herbert Walker Bush elected forty-first president on the continuum of President Reagan themes

1992—Bill Clinton elected forty-second president as a moderate (non-liberal) Democrat

1994—Republican majority elected to U.S. House for the first time in forty years

2000—George W. Bush elected forty-third president

2004—George W. Bush elected to a second term in a divided country. Forty-year cycle is complete.

2006—Republicans lose majority in U.S. House and Senate. Conservative momentum is lost.

2008—Moment of truth decision for next cycle

Chapter 2

MILESTONES ON THE JOURNEY

If we can prevent the government from wasting the
labors of the people under the pretense of taking care
of them, they must become happy.[1]

—THOMAS JEFFERSON

When Ronald Reagan delivered his "A Time for Choosing"
speech in 1964, the United States was in the throes of
debate about the philosophy of government and the extent to
which the state should be allowed to manage our lives. Most of
the issues facing us then were either local or national in scope.
The world was looking to us as a leader, but America's depen-
dence on foreign markets was still relatively small. Europe was
still trying to restructure itself after the Second World War and
find its place in the global economy. China had not yet opened
up to the West, and India and Asia were still largely undevel-
oped economically.

There were no cell phones, no laptop computers, no
advanced data networks, and no Internet. There were three
television networks: ABC, CBS, and NBC. The publicly funded

PBS network would not be established until five years later. There was no satellite television, no cable in rural areas, no fax machines, and, of course, no e-mails.

Manufacturing, transportation, automobiles, utilities, chemicals, and steel were still the big industries of the day. We were not a service economy, and the world did not demand it. The only industrial model the world had, at least since the Industrial Revolution, was the European model. The European model evolved from the landlord-tenant relationships that existed for centuries before the Industrial Revolution. There were two classes of people in that system: commoners and the nobility. Privileges were based on birth. Opportunity was not only managed, it was managed to maintain proper lines of birthright and social position. This was not a model the United States wanted to follow, and Ronald Reagan made that clear in his statements to the nation.

Even though individual liberty was the essential founding principle of the American republic, the concepts of free enterprise and individual liberty have not always been an easy sell. Yes, America has had elements of both from our earliest days, primarily through the spirit of innovation and rugged individualism that emerged naturally during the process of westward expansion. Small towns developed around the trading posts and railheads, and commerce followed the railroads across the continent. But as the nation grew in size and sophistication, the amount of government regulation began to grow as well.

Following World War II and the reconstruction of Europe, which was accomplished in large measure through the European Recovery Program known as the Marshall Plan, with U.S. economic and technical assistance to sixteen war-torn countries, bureaucrats in Washington began saying it was time for this country to begin the move toward a managed economy. The idea was to establish a controlled economy administered by a strong central government, similar to the systems in Britain and Scandinavia. Then as now, advocates of that system did not understand what it would mean for this country to give up our heritage of free enterprise. But thanks to the resistance of a few stalwarts who do understand, it hasn't happened yet.

PRESSURE FROM THE LEFT

During the 1930s, when both Europe and America were suffering through the darkest days of the Great Depression, British economist John Maynard Keynes argued that full employment could not be maintained by a free-market economy without high taxes and a broad-based welfare program to aid those on the bottom rungs of the ladder. What he proposed was a system that depended upon constantly increasing taxes and a large and impersonal bureaucracy churning out endless reports and regulations.

Despite the inherent dangers of his theories, Keynes nevertheless insisted that businesses could be managed and regulated by bureaucrats with little or no actual business experience better than by the men and women on the job who actually understood the markets. He believed that government was the true engine of prosperity. By engaging in deficit spending during times of recession and allowing a budget surplus to accumulate during times of inflation, Keynes said, business cycles could be controlled from afar and the chances of a large-scale market collapse, like the one in 1929, could be avoided.

Keynes's ideas would become the centerpiece of Franklin Roosevelt's policies during the Depression years, and they eventually gave rise to Lyndon Johnson's Great Society programs and the welfare schemes of the 1970s and 1980s. However, it became clear early on that federal regulation was putting a choke hold on business, and some economists pointed out that most of the actual cash coming out of Washington was going to program administrators and their legions of hired "experts" instead of the individuals for whom the federal assistance was intended.

Richard Nixon was elected president in 1968. His secretary of the treasury was former Texas governor John Connally, who invoked price controls. This was yet another blow to the free-market system, and it didn't work. It seemed that cabinet secretaries and members of Congress in those days couldn't bring themselves to trust the imagination and innovation of the average business owner, but the people weren't easily fooled. When Nixon ran against George McGovern in 1972, Senator McGovern proposed giving a thousand-dollar cash bonus to every American. That was just one of the proposals that convinced voters this former director of the international Food for Peace program was not their man. McGovern was soundly rejected and Nixon was reelected in a landslide.

Ronald Reagan started something in 1964 that sounded a responsive chord in the American psyche, and little by little over the next several years a dynamic new force began to emerge. The New Right and Christian Right movements were beginning to stir. No one in Washington or New York saw them coming. No one did anything to nurture them at first. The movements grew from grassroots efforts by individuals and small groups in the states and were not part of any organized effort. The organizers were individuals who were loyal to the ideas they had heard from Ronald Reagan in 1964, and they believed they could do something to help bring those views into the political arena.

Republicans suffered a major defeat in the 1974 midterm elections, due in large part to the overwhelming sense of disappointment among conservatives in the wake of the Watergate fiasco. As often happens when there is an obvious breach of trust between Washington and the electorate, large numbers of Republican voters simply stayed home. It's true that media pressures, the lingering effects of the sixties counterculture revolution, and disappointment with Republican incumbents were all factors in the debacle, but a lot of people were seeking a new direction, and a lot of them were fed up with Congress.

Republican officials had not supported the concept of less government and more freedom as they had promised. What the voters truly wanted was more control over their own lives, to make decisions for themselves and their families without the outstretched hand of government intruding into every decision. Elected officials in both parties repeatedly underestimated the wisdom and the independent spirit of the people they served. They failed to understand that the people of this country want freedom more than anything, and they will express their displeasure at the polls for anyone who doesn't get the message.

THE SPIRIT OF INDEPENDENCE

It's odd that so many of our elected officials have such a hard time embracing the main philosophy that animates the American electorate. For the first 174 years of this nation's history, we were completing the process of Manifest Destiny. We were stretching our borders and the boundaries of the imagination. Pioneers explored and settled new territories, added new states, and opened up a wide range of new possibilities. There were no limits to what we could accomplish, and the approach of the American bicentennial in 1976, celebrating two hundred years of "liberty and justice for all," was a landmark to be cherished.

When new territories were added, including statehood for Hawaii and Alaska in 1959, residents and settlers in those places weren't looking to government for their livelihood. They did not turn to the government as their primary source of goods and services. They depended upon themselves, their families, and their communities for their prosperity and well-being. Even during the darkest days of the Great Depression, most Americans were reluctant to accept charity. This was a nation that had earned its way, and there were many who refused government handouts unless they were given the opportunity to work for their pay.

When Franklin Roosevelt introduced the New Deal in 1933, the nation was suffering. In his first hundred days in office, the president called Congress into emergency session and pushed through fifteen separate pieces of legislation, creating dozens of federal programs administered by the so-called Alphabet Agencies. These included the CCC, WPA, FHA, FDIC, SEC, NLRB, REA, TVA, SSA, and many more. It was the single biggest transformation of government in American history, and it led to massive changes in public and political institutions.

In her new book, *The Forgotten Man: A New History of the Great Depression*, financial columnist Amity Shlaes makes a strong case for the view that Roosevelt's programs actually prolonged the Depression and that men and women who sought to help one another solve their own problems were forgotten in the process. Rather than providing solutions to the nation's economic woes, government's heavy-handed intervention and taxpayer-funded relief efforts actually extended the depth and severity of the Depression and short-circuited the natural processes of recovery.[2]

By providing assistance to the millions of Americans who had lost their jobs during the Depression, however, Roosevelt was seen by many as the friend of the common man, even though he was a member of the East Coast liberal establishment. But putting people to work was a master stroke, which led to the formation of a new coalition made up of blue-collar workers and urban liberals in Roosevelt's party, as well as a twenty-year run in both the White House and Congress. It was during those years that the Democratic Party earned its reputation as the party of social activism and liberal welfare programs.[3]

DIVINE RIGHTS AND WRONGS

We can debate whether or not government intervention reduced or exaggerated the impact of the Depression, but from the beginning the mind-set of the American people was not to look to government as their savior but to solve the problem by their own initiative and innovation. This is still the primary difference between American and European society. European society evolved over hundreds of years from an agrarian economy. There were essentially two classes of people: land-owners and those who worked the land. In order for the landed gentry to maintain their privileges, serfs and common laborers were needed to work the land. And keeping the lower classes in their place was essential if the aristocracy expected to maintain their status.

The king and the aristocracy provided food and shelter for the working people as they saw fit. They gave the people what they felt they needed rather than what they may have wanted. There was little or no freedom as we know it today because that would have challenged the status quo. Monarchs and feudal lords tried to justify this by saying it was the natural order of things. It was God's will, and for that matter the king was God's representative on Earth.

The French today claim their country is the birthplace of the nation-state. The emperor Charlemagne was the first ruler to label the people of a certain region in nationalistic terms and to form an entire society around that cultural identity. Whether or not the French were actually the first is not important. However, it wasn't until the first nation-states were established that the institutions of modern society would come into being. Law, literature, science, education, and the arts developed in the capitals of Europe, but the underlying structure of government in each of those countries was a land-based agrarian economy. The principle that government exists to take care of the people is a political concept that still influences policy matters in Europe today.

One of the most important early works declaring the inherent freedom of all men and natural limits on the authority of kings and rulers was the book *Lex, Rex, or the Law and the Prince*, published in 1644 by the brilliant Scottish cleric Samuel Rutherford. That work called for limited government and constitutionalism and influenced the writings of later thinkers such as Thomas Hobbes and John Locke. The book was also well known to Thomas Jefferson and John Adams and had a profound influence on the political systems established by the American Founders.[4]

Rutherford's message outraged the nobility of his day and led to his being banished and even sentenced to death—a fate he conveniently avoided by dying of natural causes. But the importance of individual liberty and decentralized authority was not lost on the men and women who built this nation. The United States of America was born from the blood, sweat, and tears of extraordinary people, who were driven by belief in their inalienable right to freedom, granted by the Creator.

That belief was a part of their DNA, put there by God Himself. Furthermore, they knew instinctively that this right was not granted by any king, government, or royal decree. They trusted in themselves and they worked for the common good. After many years of labor and hardship, they understood that free men could act collectively for the greater good of the commonwealth. They also believed that they could trust the individuals in their communities to be innovative and do the right things for the prosperity and safety of all.

The common code of moral judgment was the Bible, and these early Americans were by both nature and custom a religious people. John Adams had said, "We have no government armed with power capable of contending with human passions unbridled by morality and religion,"[5] and they knew this to be true. When the Continental Congress completed its task in 1789, Adams declared that, "Our Constitution was made only for a moral and religious people. It is wholly inadequate to the government of any other."[6] And no one questioned the rightness of the statement.

THE SPIRIT OF SELF-DETERMINATION

The founders of our nation believed that regulation was inferior to independence and innovation. There was no need to seek permission from government if they wanted to clear a forest glade to build a home; what good is government when there's real work to be done? When you're standing on the frontier with your family and there are trees growing where you want to lay out your field, what's needed is strength, courage, and a good, sharp ax. They didn't need rules. They only needed a chance to build a life and feed their families, and everything else was merely an obstacle to be overcome.

Over the years historians have argued about why the first Americans risked their lives to come to this continent. Life in the wild was more dangerous than anyone living today can begin to imagine, but they came and fought through unimaginable adversity to build a free nation. It's apparent from the documents they created, such as the Mayflower Compact, the Northwest Ordinance, and the various colonial charters, that the first settlers came for religious freedom. Some of today's academics have argued that the second and third waves of settlers came for land and business opportunities. Some came no doubt to escape servitude or inferior birthrights or unjust imprisonment. But one thing is certain: they did not come because they wanted the government to provide for their every need.

They knew the risks and they accepted them. This is the

fundamental difference between the people of the United States and the people living in the rest of the world. The Pilgrims were common, decent people who wanted to practice their faith without restraint and to live in a relationship with government that allowed them to be free. In Europe, that was not possible. Of all the things that have been said about religion in this country, to say that the Pilgrims didn't come here for religious freedom is an absolute misapplication of the facts.

The image of the Pilgrims and other settlers crossing deadly seas in those tiny boats is absolutely stunning. We can't begin to imagine what they endured. And they did it because they believed they would have the right of self determination without the king or Parliament looking over their shoulder. They were driven by their belief in freedom and opportunity. The price they paid to establish that cultural identity in this country, at such great risk to their lives and such great sacrifice to their families, must not be forgotten. It's essential for our own generation to remember those things and pass them on to our children.

But beyond that image, we must also understand how drastic a change it was for the patriots of 1776 to conceive and establish the Constitution of the United States of America as the benchmark in governing the affairs of men and as a document that would serve as the foundation of all our laws from that time to this. It's mind-boggling to think about, and their faithful labors changed everything. A government "of the people, by the people, and for the people," in Abraham Lincoln's famous phrase, would have been anathema to the ruling classes of Europe, but it was our ancestors' driving passion.

But there is another fundamental concept in the establishment of this country that is undeniable: the Founding Fathers and those who followed them believed that the right to life, liberty, and the pursuit of happiness was a God-given right that was beyond challenge and could not be abridged by claims of nobility or the divine right of kings. Their rights could not be diluted or directed by kings or parliaments, and this was the second greatest confrontation they had with the ruling mind-set of the day. The ideas that dominated the old world order were ancient, while the ideas that empowered the patriots, from Lexington to Yorktown, were truly revolutionary. They understood that the idea of a republican democracy was risky, but they believed it was vital to the future success of this great land.

Because of these remarkable beginnings, the United States of America has stood as an island of freedom in a sea of governments of unrighteous, hidden agendas. Whether it is civil war in Sudan, military control in Pakistan, or the rise of Socialist totalitarianism in Venezuela, the idea that governments must control the people rather than trust them to act in their own best interest is still the dominant ideology in much of the world today. Ronald Reagan reminded us of the guiding principles of this nation as envisioned by the founders. In so doing, he struck a resonant chord in the hearts of millions who still believed in those ideals and longed for a new birth of freedom.

A MORAL MAJORITY

In 1974 the nation was still in the wake of Depression-era reasoning, and neither the Democrats nor the Republicans had delivered on the promise of limited government. In 1975, however, the grass roots began taking matters in their own hands. They began to organize around their core beliefs of religious liberty and independence. They didn't know if their efforts would be successful, but they wanted to perpetuate for their children's future the same opportunities they had inherited from their forebears—the right to pursue happiness as they saw fit.

The New Right, the Christian Right, and the new economic supply-side Right were bound politically by their mutual interest in personal liberty. They trusted in the innovation of individuals rather than regulations and government control. They weren't afraid of their new comrades in arms because they saw no conflict in the mission statements of any of those groups. This was the coalition that went looking for Ronald Reagan even before they knew him. Reagan was a charismatic leader who believed as they did that the foundations of liberty were dependent upon a government that served the people rather than itself.

Ultimately, the most vital component of this new coalition was the Christian Right. The evangelical movement started out as a group of pastors from California who were tired of being ridiculed by the liberals and the country-club Republicans. The sentiment in political circles at the time was that evangelicals were a vocal but powerless minority who believed in superstitious fables that had no practical value in today's world. It would take courage and perseverance for those Christian leaders to continue their efforts when the party's elite were so callous in their isolation. But that was a risk they were willing to take.

Just as the idea of freedom and self-determination had threatened the established order in Europe two centuries before, the idea that God rules in the affairs of men, as the founders had believed, was an affront to the sophisticated sensibilities of the power brokers in their own party who believed they possessed all the wisdom necessary for governing the affairs of men. And in some places, that debate is just as intense today as it was at that time.

Nevertheless, those faithful believers refused to give up. Long odds were of no concern, and they were prepared to struggle alone if they had to. But little did they know the actual extent and depth of the support in the nation for their point of view. There were, in fact, millions of evangelical Christians and pro-family Roman Catholics looking for leaders they could trust, but until that time no one had yet identified the Christian Right as an actual movement. I met some of these courageous leaders when I ran Pat Robertson's campaign for president in 1988, and they were truly impressive.

I had been a national political consultant for twelve years at that time. Operating in several states, I had watched the various conservative movements develop from their inception. I encouraged all of them as best I could—I believed that the people should tell the party what they wanted rather than the party telling them what it wanted. And I began seeing a new level of energy and enthusiasm in the emerging but not yet galvanized Reagan coalition.

The Christian Right began as a grassroots movement in the states. They were identified as the Moral Majority and were eventually organized under that name by Jerry Falwell. They became a fact of mainstream politics during Pat Robertson's run for the White House. Robertson, by the strength of his presentations and his ability to mobilize large numbers of conservative voters, gave Christian activists credibility in the political marketplace. Yet, despite his strong showing, the intelligentsia was in denial—as they usually are.

In late August of 1987, it was clear from the research we had done that 33 percent of the American electorate were self-identified, born-again, evangelical Christians. Now, this is a term that no one would self-select by mistake. To call yourself a born-again Christian means you've thought about the meaning of that term, and it's a description with which you readily identify. When we asked people to identify their affinity groups on various surveys and forms, they were given either a list of terms to choose from or a space to fill in the blank, and fully one-third of all the individuals who completed those forms identified themselves as born-again Christians. This percentage has been confirmed by numerous independent research firms since that time, but in 1987 the national news media still did not grasp the size and scope of the movement. But they would soon find out.[7]

AWAKENING THE BASE

On one occasion, I was called to a meeting with a well-known national journalist with whom I had a good relationship. He told me he was leaving for the Labor Day weekend, but before going he wanted to know if I had any political activities planned over the holiday that he could include in his column. I was delighted to accommodate him. I told him what we had planned, although I said I didn't think it would be important national news. Then we spoke briefly about Pat Robertson's campaign strategy and where I thought the race was headed. I said I thought that what Robertson was doing, by bringing evangelicals and pro-family Roman Catholics into the political mainstream, was the most important thing happening in politics.

To my surprise, the columnist responded by saying, "Well, I suppose that's nice, Marc. But how many Christians can there be anyway?" He thought the number would probably be between 5 and 15 percent at most. Like a lot of people in the media, he thought Christians were a marginal force on the outside looking in. So I gave him a quick rundown of the numbers I'd seen and explained that, at a minimum, 33 percent of the electorate were self-identified born-again Christians.

But no sooner had those words left my mouth than he erupted. "Marc Nuttle, I've known you for years. You've always been a good analyst and information broker. In all these years I've never known you to overreach, but now you're manipulating the data to justify your position!" Frankly, I was shocked at his reaction. I didn't understand his anger, but I was also surprised he hadn't read the stories about the emerging conservative base in his own publication.

When I told him that the national polls and surveys, including those in his own newspaper, were showing essentially the same thing, he became even angrier and called me a liar. Now, I've been called a lot of things in my time, but never a liar. That's a sacred thing with me because it's one of the two of the Ten Commandments that my father stressed most of all. So, at that point, I pushed back from the table and said, "We've been friends a long time, and I've always trusted you as a fair and nonpartisan journalist. But I resent those words. If you have any character at all, you will apologize to me before this campaign is over—not because you feel bad about what you said, but because the facts themselves will humble you." And with that, we ended our conversation.

In January 1988, Pat Robertson defeated the sitting vice president of the United States, George Bush, in the Iowa caucuses. It was a huge triumph for Pat and the organizers of the evangelical movement, working under the leadership of Marlene Elwell. All of a sudden we were all doing interviews on a stage with two hundred fifty microphones. By the time I had finished the last one, with CNN, it was close to three o'clock in the morning, and the columnist who had called me a liar waited patiently until all the other media had left. As I began to gather my belongings, I looked around and saw that it was just he and I standing there alone in that big auditorium.

As I walked over to him and reached out my hand, he said, "Marc, I am a good man, and I do have character, whatever you may think. And I have to admit now that you were right and I was wrong. I didn't want to believe that the Christian base even existed in the United States. And I'm sorry I called you a liar." I looked at him and said, "Thank you. Done, forgiven, forgotten." From that moment we resumed our former good relationship.

THE BIRTH OF A MOVEMENT

Throughout their long journey, the Christian Right remained loyal and consistent in their beliefs and principles. They had been a big part of the coalition that made the right decisions in 1975 to stay the course that Ronald Reagan had laid out in 1964. In the presidential cycle of 1976, the Christian Right had not yet been forged into a cohesive movement, but Pat Robertson's campaign completed the process in 1988. Pat actually came in first or second in the first six primaries that year. Most of them were caucus states, but he really showed his broad appeal in the state of Washington. Pat ultimately captured 288 delegates to the national convention. But more importantly, his organization took over thirty state parties, much to the surprise of local politicians. And that was a good thing.

The political establishment learned two important things that year: First, in society, Christians are no different than anyone else. They were not radioactive; they represented every profession, background, and ethnic group. They were good participants in committee meetings for budget, finance, and rules. And second, the establishment learned that evangelical voters were a natural fit into their coalition. New Right conservatives and economic supply-side conservatives had no problem with them personally or with their beliefs. There was little or no tension in the coalition.

So these movements that began with the inspiration of Ronald Reagan and morphed into the Reagan coalition peaked in their cohesion in the 2004 presidential cycle, exactly forty years after it all began. Republican-elected officials, however, have made some of the same mistakes that Republican leaders made in 1974. They did not build confidence within the base by their actions. After the first few years of control, the Republican-controlled Congress appeared to be unaccountable. They were not policing their own. Deficits were out of control, and commitment to core spiritual beliefs was compromised. In 2006, as in 1974, Republicans suffered a great defeat, losing both the House and the Senate. So today the grass roots is once again looking for leadership and reconstituting itself, just as it did after that off-year election.

The difference this time is that the movement is reorganizing and strengthening itself, not starting from scratch. In 1976, the Reagan coalition was unprepared to make an impact. Now, in 2008, no one individual has emerged as the clear choice of the people, but the conservative coalition is prepared to make an impact. The big issue in 2008 is whether or not we will move toward more government control and a managed society, as the Democratic candidates have proposed, or pick up again and move toward the society that Ronald Reagan described. If we fail to make the right choices this time, we will get a government that believes in Europeanization and will, whether we like it or not, take that dreaded first step toward the "[one] thousand years of darkness" Reagan referred to in his speech.

Former Speaker of the House Newt Gingrich has been articulate in his discussions of how the Republican Congress abandoned their mission. Along with Mickey Edwards, the former congressman from Oklahoma, Gingrich is calling for a return to the commitment and principles of freedom enunciated by the original Reagan coalition. These principles are centered in the belief that solutions can be found for all our problems if we will trust the resourcefulness and innovation of the American people. "Power to the People" is not just an axiom of the sixties; it's the best way to ensure that reason and respect will prevail rather than a centralized government in the hands of liberal social planners.

THE CHALLENGE BEFORE US

It is my hope that the Christian Right will not abandon the cause. There are many powerful forces that would love to shove them to the sidelines, but we cannot afford to let that happen. What we want more than anything is less government interference in our lives. Bigger government and centralized control of the economy can only result in the Europeanization of America and all the failures that go with it. Europe was once the most religious society in the world; it is now one of the least religious. And I would submit that the correlation between the economic decline of Europe and the moral and spiritual decline are not coincidental.

The grass roots in the United States today is realigning itself along new lines. There are new movements emerging among Christian activists. Some of the younger leaders are motivated by their concern for issues such as poverty, the AIDS epidemic, and the environment. Their ideas may not be yours, but they're not inconsistent with the ideals of the Founding Fathers or of Ronald Reagan. Individual liberty and limited government offer the best opportunity for innovation in all of these areas.

At the same time, the New Right is staking out their position on issues such as globalism, immigration, terrorism, and the challenges brought about by the rise of China and other third-world economies. My old colleague, Paul Weyrich, has written a series of articles in recent months under the heading, "The Next Conservatism." In them, he argues that we must define the results we want from our political institutions. The cultural war, he says, is just as important as the war on terrorism or the battles between Democrats and Republicans at the polls, and I believe he's right about that. It means nothing for our side to control Congress if it does not result in the survival of the culture that we want for our children.

It's no mistake that the United States is the most religious nation on the earth and that we maintain strict separation of church and state. Government does nothing to advocate or support religion, yet religion still thrives in this country. This is a paradox for most Europeans today; they don't understand how the people of such a powerful, wealthy, sophisticated nation can worship God in such formidable numbers. But they also don't understand that they caused it.

The men and women who came to these shores from Europe in the seventeenth and eighteenth centuries were looking for freedom—freedom from government and all the antiquated systems designed to keep them in service to the ruling elite. The fact that they came, that they survived, that they were able to establish any nation at all, and that from the most unlikely beginnings they created the greatest economic and military power in the history of mankind was nothing short of a miracle. In that knowledge, our forefathers found their true calling and purpose in life; so why wouldn't they want to worship the Creator who had led them on such a magnificent journey?

Chapter 3

RELIGIOUS TOLERANCE IN REVERSE

*America stands for liberty, for the pursuit of happiness,
and for the unalienable right for life. This right to life
cannot be granted or denied by government because
it does not come from government, it comes from the
Creator of life.*[1]

—GEORGE W. BUSH

Apparently it's difficult for some people to understand just
how unique the government of the United States truly is.
Many people mistakenly believe that the Supreme Court is the
supreme law of the land. It is not. Yes, it is the supreme arbiter
of the law and rulings on points of law that can affect our interpretation of the Constitution. The Supreme Court is only one
of three equal branches of government—judicial, legislative,
and executive—and rulings handed down by the Court must be
based on a particular set of facts and restricted to the particular cases brought before them.

The Constitution is the supreme law of the land from which all the powers of government derive. This power is controlled and limited only by the will of the people as they decide how the government ought to serve their interests and provide for their needs. In their wisdom, the Founding Fathers gave us three branches of government, with checks and balances between them so that no one branch could dominate the others. Federal judges are nominated by the president and confirmed by the Senate to serve in the nation's federal courts. They are appointed for life and are required to be faithful interpreters of the law based on the Constitution. By design these judges have no legislative, executive, or fiduciary authority.

Judges who serve in America's courts are expected to be well informed in all areas of jurisprudence. They are to be individuals of impeccable character, circumspect in their personal behavior, and defenders of the common good. They are empowered to settle disputes and resolve legal controversies according to existing case law. They are not empowered to go beyond the Constitution and legal precedent or to render judgments based on their own personal opinions. Consequently, justices of the Supreme Court and judges in all the other federal courts are dependent on the executive and legislative branches. The judicial branch is equal to the other branches, and it is nevertheless subject to the will of the people through the electoral process and the selection of the legislature and the chief executive.

The key principle to be remembered is that the Constitution of the United States demands full faith and allegiance of every citizen, including lawmakers, public servants, and those in any position of authority. Unless modified by an amendment passed by Congress and ratified by the states, the Constitution as it exists today is the final authority on what may and may not be done in matters of law. And when any man or woman stands for election in this country, it is understood that they are bound by the fundamental laws and principles contained in the Constitution.

There are many implications of these facts. Certainly, religious liberty is at the top of the list. But a relatively new issue has emerged in the presidential arena in recent months. The question is, how should the religious beliefs of a candidate for the nation's highest office affect the decision of whom to support? It's especially interesting that we're asking this question today, exactly forty years after Ronald Reagan set the general guidelines for the modern conservative movement. Most people believed we had dealt with this issue when John Kennedy delivered his famous speech to the Southern Baptists in 1960. But clearly the debate is still not settled.

Today the question is whether or not the Mormon beliefs of former presidential candidate Mitt Romney ought to be a matter of concern. The issue was much easier to deal with when it was the Catholic question. The Catholic church was then, and still is, the largest denomination in the country. The church supports schools, hospitals, and day-care centers, and provides many vital social services. It has an august history dating back to the origins of the Christian church in the second and third century and is acclaimed internationally for its high academic standards. The public's concern in 1960 wasn't the legitimacy of the Catholic faith, but whether or not Mr. Kennedy's allegiance would be to the pope or to the Constitution of the United States.

The questions concerning Governor Romney's Mormon beliefs are somewhat more complex than the ones that faced Jack Kennedy. Many Christians question the legitimacy of the Mormon religion. While the official name of the denomination is the Church of Jesus Christ of Latter-Day Saints, many consider Mormonism a cult, and Romney's critics point to fundamental doctrinal differences between Mormon teachings and historical Christianity. In general, however, most people don't really know much about Mormon teachings. The Mormon church operates worldwide but is headquartered in Utah, which is where the largest concentration of Mormon faithful are to be found. Almost without exception, members of this denomination describe themselves as Christians, but that doesn't settle the matter.

WHOM DO YOU TRUST?

Perhaps we need to consider another approach. Whenever I'm trying to make an important decision in my own life, I will generally stop to think about how the decision will affect my family, my associates, and my calling as a Christian. I have often done this with regard to my involvement in politics and the electoral process. How will the choices I make affect those important relationships? Even though Jesus wasn't directly involved in politics, He certainly shook up the political establishment of His day. He challenged their authority and made it clear that His Word was the truth. At the same time, He did not advocate overthrowing the government and never suggested the Roman Empire should be Christianized.

The scripture we hear so often is, "Render to Caesar the things that are Caesar's, and to God the things that are God's" (Mark 12:17). The apostle Paul says, "Do you want to be unafraid of the authority? Do what is good, and you will have praise from the same" (Rom. 13:3). What both of these passages tell us is that our relationship with government is a two-way street. Government exists to provide for the common good and to defend the interests of the people. Consequently, it is our Christian duty to obey the laws that are established for our good. We also have an obligation to hold government accountable and demand that the law serve the people's interests. But we must not forget that our first and highest allegiance is to God.

The Christian's purpose with regard to government is to maintain a healthy balance in what we seek from government and what we produce by our own initiative. It's imperative that free people strive to keep government as their servant and not their master. Those who rely exclusively on government for their personal welfare will end up as slaves of the state. When government has the authority to take away your freedom and your ability to make your own decisions independently, you inevitably end up in a "spiritual prison."

One of our goals as conservatives is to help people maintain this sense of balance so they will have the freedom to pursue their goals as they see fit. Anyone who becomes dependent on government for their daily sustenance will find it impossible to ignore government's demands, even when it involves something that may be a fundamental violation of their faith. This is one of the main reasons why the founders of our nation insisted upon freedom from government interference in matters of faith and why religious liberty is the very first principle addressed by the First Amendment. One of the tenets of modern conservatism is to help our fellow citizens avoid entanglements with government that could destroy their souls.

In that context, then, the question to be asked is, what do you seek from government in this system of things? Should your analysis of a candidate's values and his or her appropriateness for holding public office be measured by whether or not he or she agrees with your moral values? Should he or she also subscribe to the particular tenets of your religious faith? Or should he or she, on the other hand, subscribe to the principles enshrined in the United States Constitution and the view that government is to be the servant of the people and is, by law, restricted from *establishing* any particular religious doctrine or interfering in the *free exercise* of our religious beliefs?

With these questions in mind, could you vote for a Jewish person for president? If the candidate affirms their support for the Constitution and the law and expresses their belief in your moral and political positions, what's to stop you? I would argue that it should not matter whether the person is a Jew, a Mormon, a Southern Baptist, or an Anglican. But some will say Jews, Baptists, and Anglicans are not a cult, and Mormons are. If you feel strongly about that, you're entitled to your opinion, and you're free to make your choice at the polls. But you need to understand that this is a spiritual question, not a political one.

THE PROPER ROLE OF GOVERNMENT

The New Testament never disqualifies the government of Rome, even though the Romans were pagans and Caesar declared himself to be God. The Romans did not worship the God of Abraham; they were not even monotheistic. Yet, Jesus told His followers to pay their taxes, as requested. This can only mean that the administration of government is valuable and appropriate to society.

Now, I am not a Libertarian. I believe that government serves an important role in the affairs of a nation, administering our laws. However, I want that role to be the one that "we the people" give it, and not whatever the lawmakers and bureaucrats might prefer. I like the fact that my streets are paved. It gives me comfort to know that there is an emergency room in my city. I'm happy to know that the meal I ate for lunch today was inspected, both before it came to the restaurant and in the kitchen where it was prepared.

I'm also grateful to know that the medicine I took this morning was inspected and approved by the U.S. Food and Drug Administration. The men and women serving in Iraq, Afghanistan, and many other places around the world are a blessing, protecting our homeland and risking their lives for our safety. There are police, firemen, air traffic controllers, and many others who serve the public interest as part of an integrated system of federal, state, and local governments, and I thank God for all of them. Nothing I believe as a Christian prevents me from supporting those individuals or the institutions they serve, even though I know practically nothing about what they may believe or where they may worship.

Any differences I may have with the Mormon religion are personal, spiritual issues. These differences are involved in another realm or in the life hereafter, which has no direct impact on government in this system of things. But no one is demanding that I subscribe to Mormonism any more than John Kennedy demanded that I convert to Catholicism. Furthermore, I know of no differences that I have with the men and women of that faith, in the operation of the government's business, that would prevent me from casting my vote for someone of that persuasion.

I would say much the same about other religions as well, with the exception of Islam. Islamic law makes no place for religious tolerance. As we've learned only too well over the past several years, certain Muslim leaders insist that teachings of the Quran and the application of Sharia must dominate the affairs of state. The doctrine of separation of church and state contained in our own constitutional system is not acceptable to Islamic fundamentalists. They do not recognize religious pluralism, which puts them in conflict with the U.S. Constitution. Any Muslim running for federal office would have to explain, with absolute certainty, what their position is on conflict of interest of being loyal to their faith and loyal to the Constitution.

When Mitt Romney addressed the issue of the separation of church and state at the George Bush Presidential Library Museum, he said that if he were elected president of the United States, he would serve only the American people. He said:

> As Governor [of Massachusetts], I tried to do right as best I
> knew it, serving the law and answering to the Constitution.

> I did not confuse the particular teachings of my church
> with the obligations of the office and of the Constitution—
> and, of course, I would not do so as President. I will put no
> doctrine of any church above the plain duties of the office
> and the sovereign authority of the law.[2]

In my opinion, every disciple of a major religion ought to be able to make the same claim that Governor Romney made in that speech, declaring full faith and allegiance to the Constitution. The key to maintaining a position of religious tolerance in government's sea of hidden agendas is absolute commitment to the Constitution, which sets forth the rights of the people and the responsibilities of government to serve our needs.

No one in the Vatican has said that the United States of America must become a Catholic nation. No one from the Southern Baptist Convention is demanding that the United States become a Baptist nation. No rabbinical official in Jerusalem, no elder of the Mormon church in Salt Lake City, and no spokesperson for any of the Christian denominations is saying that the United States must give up its religious neutrality to endorse any of those faiths.

I'm sure there are ayatollahs and imams in the world today who would demand that all nations either convert to Islam or perish by the sword. Consequently, any Muslim running for the office of president of the United States would have a much greater burden of proof regarding how he would uphold the Constitution without breaching the principle of separation of church and state. For the moment at least, that's not a problem. But we need to understand that the other side of religious tolerance is religious neutrality. If we prohibit government from interfering in our private religious practices, then we cannot demand that individuals seeking government office subscribe to our private religious beliefs.

SOVEREIGNTY OF THE LAW

It's important not to miss the emphasis on the word *sovereign* in Governor Romney's remarks at the Bush Library. Everyone has some value or some principle they consider to be sovereign, whether they know it or not. Even atheists have some sort of sovereign belief dealing with the nature of existence and how we came to be as we are. At some moment in our youth, each of us recognized that there are forces outside our control. We all got here somehow. We may not know how, exactly, but we believe in that force because the evidence is undeniable.

No one can fully explain how we came into existence. The Christian faith teaches that we were created by God for His glory, and the ancient confessions of the church hold that the chief aim of man is to glorify God and enjoy Him forever. But our physical existence is another matter. Something had to precede us.

Many secularists will argue for the big bang theory, that somehow life emerged full blown in an instant from nothing in some great cataclysmic event millions of years ago. Darwinists believe that life emerged in the primal ooze, as one single cell evolved over infinite eons from one life form to another and another and another. And all of the mind-boggling complexity and beauty of nature evolved randomly, leading ultimately to human life and the entire world as we know it. *Shazam!*

Unanswered questions taken as faith are the essence of religion. Whether in Christianity or secular humanism, the points that cannot be proven by physical evidence are taken on faith. No one has a clue how or if the big bang occurred or what preceded it. What force could have caused it, and where did all the elements come from in the first place? Scientists say it's too soon to know the answers to such questions; they'll tell us when they get all the facts. But even this sounds more like religion than science. Something or someone came before us and has always existed; the only debate is what or who that something or someone may be.

The word *sovereign* denotes something to which we ascribe supreme rank or importance in our system of values. In what do you place your ultimate trust? In Mitt Romney's speech cited above, he said his commitment was to the duties of the office and the "sovereign authority of the law," both of which are clearly defined by the Constitution of the United States. The law, as the Declaration of Independence attests, is based on the eternal truth "that all men are created equal, that they are endowed by their Creator with certain unalienable Rights, that among these are Life, Liberty, and the pursuit of Happiness."[3]

In October 2006, more than a year before his visit to the Bush Library, Romney met with fifteen evangelical leaders, including Jerry Falwell, Franklin Graham, Richard Land of the Southern Baptist Convention, and others, for an informal but pointed discussion of his religious beliefs. As reported by *Newsweek* magazine, the men talked over soup and sandwiches, with the goal of finding out whether or not they could support Romney's candidacy if he decided to run for president in 2008.

Dr. Richard Lee, a Baptist minister from Georgia, cut to the chase and asked Romney what he actually believed about Jesus Christ. The governor replied, "When I say Jesus Christ is my Lord and Savior, I realize that means something different to you than it does to me." But he asked the Christian leaders to remember that they all shared the belief that Jesus Christ was born of a virgin, was crucified, and rose again after three days.[4]

Richard Lee joked, "So you're really a Baptist!" But despite the pause for comic relief, the evangelical leaders were apparently satisfied with the governor's assurances that, like John Kennedy before him, his religion beliefs and his political interests were separate matters. If Christians expect religious tolerance from others, it's only fair that we practice what we preach—to the extent that tolerance doesn't compromise our own values and beliefs. There's no question that the first Christians practiced their faith, despite the persecutions they endured, by simply obeying the law of the land, as Christ and the apostles had instructed them to do.

CHOOSING LEADERS WE TRUST

As we think about all the issues that can arise in the course of a political campaign, it would be helpful to have some way of measuring the candidates in order to evaluate their positions on the issues. How does one decide which issues are critical in selecting the right man or woman for office? We might begin by asking: What is government forcing me to do today that's in violation of my basic rights and beliefs? Can government force me to have an abortion? Is government forcing anyone in my family to be a homosexual? Is government threatening to take away my children in order to educate them as they see fit? If the answer to these questions is no, then what is it we want to change about the way government works?

In China, where there's a limit on the number of children a family can have, a pregnant mother may be forced to have an abortion. In Communist countries, children can be taken away from their parents and educated however the state sees fit. As United States citizens, we are free to educate our children in the public school system, in private schools, or in a home school. As a free, democratic nation, we demand that kind of flexibility, and it's a privilege that is constitutionally guaranteed.

On the other hand, the government can increase taxes to an intolerable level, or they can mandate benefits to the employees of your business that are so costly they can put you out of business. Government can overinspect, overregulate, and overcontrol. Nothing is more dangerous to our freedoms than a government agency on the prowl. But the determining factor may be simpler than you think: do you believe in government control, or do you believe in limited government?

Most of the issues in the political debate today come down to this: Do we want to extend the laws that exist or retract them? Do we want more regulation or less? And whom do you trust to do the right thing for this country: government bureaucrats equipped with writs and regulations, or the innovation of the American people equipped with the foundation of freedom?

One way to find the candidates who give you the greatest sense of comfort and trust is to construct a grid. In fact, I would suggest you may want to do this exercise yourself. At the top of a blank sheet of paper, make a list of some of the important moral principles that government does *not* force you to violate. In other words, list some of the issues that are very important to you and your family in which government does not force upon you. These are government issues that would force you to become a pilgrim and leave the country.

Next, list some of the issues over which government does have authority and can command compliance. Some of these issues are, in fact, being debated in the current election cycle. After that, list some of the issues that must be addressed as a society, for our children's future, that would come within the purview of government. Then, finally, list some of the issues outside our control that we must at some point deal with as a nation. Here's an example of how these various lists might look:

Government action that would make me a pilgrim:	Government ALLOWS me to:
• Force me to have an abortion	• Educate my children as I see fit
• Force me to recognize or enter into gay marriage	• Worship as I wish
• Force me to deny my religious beliefs	• Travel freely around the country

Government actions that can intrude upon my freedom:
• Taxation
• Mandated benefits: i.e., must buy or provide health insurance
• Universal unionism
• Environmental controls: i.e., carbon tax or onerous manufacturing restrictions
• Breach of personal liberties, such as surveillance
• Not enforcing immigration laws

Issues about which I must decide what I want government to do, provide or fix—what am I willing to sacrifice to allow these?

Issues requiring immediate action:	Issues requiring long-term action or plans of action (but still critical for me to consider when I make decisions about voting):
• Social Security	• Global terrorism
• Immigration	• U.S. energy independence
• Medicare/Medicaid and health care in general	• Federal government deficit spending
• Survival of U.S. small business in a world economy	• Congressional earmarks (pork barrel spending)
• Democracy and equitable governing	• The environment (safety, preservation, etc.)

THE DECISION-MAKING PROCESS

The first thing you must do in any consideration of this kind is to decide what you believe. What is your overriding view of government, and what are the limits to government intrusion beyond which you will not go? Do you believe in giving government absolute authority to solve society's problems as it sees fit, or do you believe in limited government? Clearly, the candidates of one political party believe in expanding the role and reach of government into every area of our daily lives, while the leading candidates of the other party believe that citizens know better than government how to conduct their own affairs. To make this determination, you must understand spiritually what you are *not* willing to do, no matter what the government says.

Unless you are a conscientious objector and refuse to serve your nation in time of war, there is no law on the books that I know of that if you as a Christian obey it, you will be in violation of your religious beliefs. I'm sure you would support no candidate who suggested such a law. That day may come in the future, and if it does I hope you will stand by your beliefs, just as we all will. But, thank God, that prospect is not bearing down on us at the moment.

The process I'm suggesting involves taking a look at the positions of the various contenders and asking yourself some basic questions; for example, does the answer to any problem presented by the candidate increase my freedom, impose upon my freedom, or have no impact on my freedom? Every time you allow the government to impose on your freedom, even in matters such as health, safety, and basic social services, you take one more step down the path to spiritual bondage.

Next, ask yourself: Does the position of this candidate increase my control over my own destiny? Does it allow me to work toward a better future for my family? Does it make government more accountable? Or does it let the legions of government regulators and experts hide behind their anonymity?

In Newt Gingrich's new book, *Real Change*, he deals with these and similar issues in the context of defining citizen leaders. With a series of action steps and a detailed leadership model, he discusses values, vision, metrics, strategies, and projects with an approach designed to make government smaller, more efficient, and more responsive to the people. As always, the former Speaker proves himself to be an original thinker and strategist, and this new book is certainly worth a look.[5]

Anyone familiar with American history has heard story after story about how America was the last great escape. Our forefathers gave up their comfortable lives in Europe and crossed the angry sea to escape to a land of opportunity. If they had failed in the effort to establish a constitutional democracy that guarantees freedom of opportunity, the world would have become one giant prison with no hope. That is not just a romantic retelling of our history; I believe it is true and that, as Ronald Reagan expressed it, America is the last best hope of man on the earth. Our challenge now is to find leaders who agree with that view and who are pledged to uphold the standards and traditions that made it so.

Today we have to take the lead once again, redefining who we are and what we will demand of those who hold high office in this country. The forty-year cycle that began with Reagan's speech to the Republican National Convention is now complete, and the baton has been passed to you and me, the heirs of that inspiring legacy. It is our turn to decide what sort of world we will inhabit for the next forty years. We don't have the luxury of missing this election cycle. Time is too short, and the issues are too important. A new cycle began in 2008 that, one way or the other, will change the world as we know it. What choices will we make?

Here are some of the issues and challenges that will determine what we will become:

ISSUES WE MUST FACE AS A NATION

Powerful organizations led by men
- Al Qaeda

- The third-world political attack (led by Venezuelan President Hugo Chavez)
- Socialism in general as a movement

Entities that support these threats in some ways
- World organized crime and corruption
- Tribal culture
- The United Nations

Natural collective forces
- Rise of China, economically and militarily
- Rise of India
- The Internet
- World Trade Organization
- The G8—Global Politics Network
- The EU, NAFTA, and other global agreements
- Immigration and migration driven by economic issues

The issues listed above may seem complicated. Most of us aren't accustomed to thinking in such large-scale strategic terms. But when you apply a simple standard, the decision-making process becomes a little easier. Once you define what you want, what you believe, and what you want for your children's future, then every measure of every issue may be evaluated against that standard. For example, I believe in free enterprise; then, I would not support any issue that would infringe upon the small-business owner's ability to make an honest living and succeed in that business.

My daughter owns a retail business. Her business is growing because she provides a valuable service and is good at what she does. She has six employees, who are glad to be working there. Any issue that would increase her costs to the point that she cannot stay in business would be unacceptable to me. On the other hand, she is free to decide what she can afford and what she can do, above and beyond meeting her payroll, to support the services and local customs of her community.

I will not support the expansion of any government program that does not have some type of accountability for its results. I would not be in favor of any law that does not allow a person to control the education of his or her children. And I would not be in favor of any program that prevents the United States military from pursuing its mission of protecting the interests of this country and providing for our security. The overriding principle is this: does the solution that the candidate is proposing increase or decrease my freedom?

APPLYING YOUR PERSONAL GRID

When you go through this process, you will find that no candidate currently in the race for president is proposing anything that would require you to violate your faith. My duty as a Christian, to abide by the tenets of my faith and offer a compelling witness of Christ's love, does not require any action from government. I would be strongly opposed to any law that would require me to deny my faith. But I would be equally opposed to any law that would require others to profess a belief they do not hold. What I want is an environment that allows every citizen to be free so they can make their own decisions regarding faith and values without worrying about whether or not their children will be able to eat that night.

Some might ask how that formulation applies to an issue such as abortion. Just because there's no law that says I have to abort my child, someone might say, "That doesn't mean it's OK!" My answer would be that, no, it's not OK. I believe in the Ten Commandments. This is the foundational code of Judeo-Christian faith and practice and the cornerstone of Western law for more than a thousand years. The sixth commandment says, "You shall not murder," and that certainly applies to the life of the child in the womb.

But there's a difference between a law that forces you to do something to which you object on religious and moral grounds and a law that merely allows practices to which you object. If this is a priority with you—as it is with me, I might add—then put it on your grid. This is something you can fight for through the political process, and you can use your voice and your vote to support only those candidates who are strongly against legalized abortion

But here is the critical question: If the nominee of the Democratic Party turns out to be Hillary Clinton, and had the nominee of the Republican Party been former candidate Rudy Giuliani, and both candidates are pro-choice and in favor of keeping the Supreme Court's *Roe v. Wade* ruling on the books, would that have given you a pass to sit out the election? Absolutely not. But why? Because the real issue here is not simply one bad law. The issue is freedom and what you hope to accomplish in the future.

Further, if the Republican nominee is John McCain or Ron Paul, your decision-making process would be the same. The case is identical for Barack Obama or John Edwards, had he stayed in the race. What are your priorities? What are your absolutes on values? What are your requirements for freedom?

You must determine which candidate and which party is most favorable to your Christian worldview. Which one is in favor of more and bigger government, and which one is more responsive to the concerns of the electorate? By sitting out the election, you would be leaving the future of your children and grandchildren to others who may not agree with you on any of the important issues of the day. You would be taking a chance that is totally unacceptable. In the final analysis, you must make your own choices and give your support to the candidates who are least likely to take us down the path toward a thousand years of darkness.

In this chapter we've discussed religious intolerance by religious people and how to think about faith and values in the political arena. What I'm advocating is a new way of looking at these things. The idea is to keep government issues in a separate category from faith issues. As citizens, we have a duty to deal with government and decide how the nation is to be governed. This is a privilege purchased for us by the Founding Fathers at the price of their own blood. But we live for eternity. Jesus asked, "Is not life more than food and the body more than clothing?" (Matt. 6:25). Jesus meant everything He said, and He said that His kingdom is not of this world. We make a big mistake when we confuse this earthly kingdom with the kingdom of God.

Supporting democracy and keeping America an island of freedom in a sea of hidden agendas is an important goal, and each of us can have a say in that process. Reaching the lost and bringing others into the kingdom of God is an even more important goal, and we can take part in that high calling by simply living out our faith day by day. There's no conflict in these missions. We can work for a better world here and now, and we can help build the kingdom of God. But we need to understand that they are two different things.

A TELLING EXAMPLE

In Beirut, Lebanon, partly because of religious intolerance, the democratic system is in jeopardy. The term of Lebanon's president Emile Lahood expired on November 3, 2007. The constitution of that country requires that a new Christian president be elected in rotation in a timely manner, but the Islamic revolutionary party Hezbollah boycotted the government and threw the entire process into turmoil. Prime Minister Fouad Siniora has a narrow majority. But he will need the support of Hezbollah if he hopes to confirm his election and make it legitimate. But the parties are deadlocked, and as of this writing the democratic system in that country is in peril.

The government there does not trust "the will of the people," or even their own ability to bring about a peaceful transfer of power. Unlike this country, where the Constitution spells out the precise details of the electoral process, the process there is subject at all times to the wiles of those in power. Government does not allow the people to solve their own problems and make changes at the election booth. Separation of church and state is not the same priority. As a result, democracy is in peril in that part of the world. We must never allow that sort of thing to happen in the United States of America.

Governor Mitt Romney, in his speech last December, made another important comment about our nation's history, which spoke volumes about the importance of religious tolerance and the rule of law in this nation. He said:

> Recall the early days of the first Continental Congress in Philadelphia, during the fall of 1774. With Boston occupied by British troops, there were rumors of imminent hostility and fears of an impending war. In this time of peril, someone suggested that they pray. But there were objections. They were too divided in religious sentiments, what with Episcopalians and Quakers, Anabaptists and Congregationalists, Presbyterians and Catholics.
>
> Then Sam Adams rose and said he would hear a prayer from anyone of piety and good character, as long as they were a patriot. And so together they prayed, and together they fought, and together, by the grace of God...they founded this great nation.[6]

That marvelous story says a lot about the spirit of faith and freedom that brought this nation into being. But we should also pause to recall the words of Benjamin Franklin, who was a deist and one of the most secular founders, when he addressed the Constitutional Convention in 1787 in an attempt to end the deadlock separating the various political interests in attendance. His words were eloquent and should not be forgotten. Franklin was already eighty-one years of age at the time, hard of hearing, and dependent on a sturdy cane and a strong young lad to help him get around. But he rose to his feet and spoke these words:

> I've lived, Sir, a long time, and the longer I live, the more convincing proofs I see of this truth—that God governs in the affairs of men. And if a sparrow cannot fall to the ground without his notice, is it probable that an empire can rise without his aid? We have been assured, Sir, in the sacred writings, that except the Lord build the house they labor in vain who build it. I firmly believe this—and I also believe that without his concurring aid, we shall succeed in this political building no better than the builders of Babel: We shall be divided by our little partial local interests; our projects will be confounded, and we ourselves shall become a reproach and bye-word down to future ages. And what is worse, mankind may hereafter from this unfortunate instance, despair of establishing governments by human wisdom and leave it to chance, war, and conquest. I therefore beg leave to move that henceforth prayers imploring the assistance of Heaven, and its blessing on our deliberations, be held in this assembly every morning before we proceed to business, and that one or more of the clergy of this city be requested to officiate in that service.[7]

The delegate from New Jersey, Jonathan Dayton, later reported on the reaction of the members of that body to Franklin's words. He writes that, "The Doctor sat down, and never did I behold a countenance at once so dignified and delighted as was that of Washington at the close of the address; nor were the members of the convention generally less affected. The words of the venerable Franklin fell upon our ears with a weight and authority, even greater than we may suppose an oracle to have had in a Roman senate."[8] After many long months of partisan bickering, Franklin's request was honored and prayers were made. The Constitution was signed by thirty-nine delegates on September 17, 1787, and sent to the states for ratification.

When we work through our differences to achieve reasonable ends, we show our honor for the founders who fought and died for the freedoms we enjoy today. What Dr. Franklin understood was that reason and sound political judgment were essential in the work those men were doing. But without spiritual guidance and the blessings of heaven, nothing as important as a Constitution to last for the ages could ever have been completed.

These were men of very different backgrounds, from every region of the country. There were many times when compromise was essential. But they did it, and the document they created has guided this nation for more than two hundred twenty years. British prime minister William Gladstone later described the American Constitution as "the most wonderful work ever struck off at a given time by the brain and purpose of man."[9]

There are many things to be learned from these examples, but it's worth noting that the issues we're dealing with today may be just as important to future generations as those that troubled the founders in earlier times. We can't always have everything we want, and sometimes we have to depend on the goodwill of our allies and friends. But when we've done all we can do, we want to be able to say to our children and grandchildren that we did everything we could to preserve, protect, and defend the Constitution of the United States and the freedoms it provides.

Chapter 4

THE QUALITIES OF A LEADER

*The conservative believes that there exists an enduring
moral order. That order is made for man, and man is
made for it: human nature is a constant, and moral
truths are permanent.*[1]

—RUSSELL KIRK

What are the qualities of a leader? When you're deciding
whether or not to support a candidate for public office,
what are the things you look for? Is it the individual's personality, their experience in business or politics, their position on
important social issues, or do you perhaps watch for the kinds
of endorsements they receive from people you respect? If you're
like most people, it's probably a combination of all of the above,
along with that certain feeling you get when you hear them
speak about the issues.

When your children need your advice, you will do everything you can to share with them whatever information or
knowledge you may have to help with the decisions they need
to make. You do this for no other reason than the fact that you

love them and you want them to be the best they can be. In most cases you're not concerned for yourself or for any sacrifice you may be called upon to make. You want to give your family the best information you can based on the resources at your disposal. It's selfless leadership based on love.

What greater gift could you give to your kids than your loving concern for their well-being? But beyond the attention we give to our families, we all have a peer group of some type that looks to us for information. It may be a co-worker, someone at church, a member of a volunteer or social organization you belong to, or maybe it's a stranger you've influenced without even knowing it.

In one way or another, we all look to other people for input and advice, and that's especially true when we have friends we can trust and with whom we have interests, values, and beliefs in common. You have no idea how helpful it may be to someone else when you speak to them about issues of concern, offering an honest opinion or simply discussing the issues of the day in a logical and attentive manner.

Some of us may not have the confidence to talk about controversial topics with our friends and business associates. Many people in my generation will remember a time when our parents or other close friends told us there were two subjects we must never talk about in public: politics and religion. But in light of the political situation in this country today, those are the subjects we need to be thinking and speaking about most of all.

But how do you do that? The process is not as dangerous or as complicated as most people think. You begin by defining yourself politically in the most general terms. We discussed the process briefly in the previous chapter. Once you've done that, you prioritize your interests and issues based on what's happening in the political arena at the time and to what extent moral and ethical issues may be involved. This means thinking about the things you value most and the issues that touch you most deeply.

How much government do you need to feel secure about your future? How important is that determination to your freedom? What needs to happen in society today to make the future feel safer and healthier for your children and grandchildren? Does the environment you envision require that new laws be enacted? Does it require a greater emphasis on spiritual matters? What would give you the greatest sense of satisfaction and accomplishment if you could use your influence to bring about some type of change?

GOD'S PLAN OF ORDER

We've all heard the expression, "You can't legislate morality." It's a provocative phrase, to say the least, but it's really meaningless. It's not that you can't legislate morality; it's that we shouldn't have to. As I said earlier, the entire basis of Western law rests on a moral code: the Ten Commandments. Those ten fundamental laws are nothing more or less than a handbook for a happy life. They are God's plan of order for our good.

God requires obedience to moral laws and forbids destructive behaviors, not because He's some sort of angry traffic cop, but because He cares for our well-being. Jeremiah 29:11 says, "For I know the thoughts that I think toward you, says the LORD, thoughts of peace and not of evil, to give you a future and a hope." Those are the words of a loving father, not an angry cosmic killjoy.

When you hear people complaining about the "thou shalt nots" in the commandments, you can be certain they're missing the point. God could just as easily have given us ten thousand commandments if He wanted to, but He didn't. He gave us ten basic rules to live by because He cares about us and wants the best for us. There's no question that living by those ten rules would make life better for everyone if we would only do it more often.

In his book *Courting Disaster*, Pat Robertson offers a compelling discussion of this subject and describes what has happened to the rule of law since the Ten Commandments fell into disfavor with America's lawmakers. The US Code, which is cited in virtually every case decided by the United States Supreme Court, is a compilation of all the federal statutes enacted by Congress and signed into law by the president. According to a study of the Code conducted by Professor John Baker for the Federalist Society, there are at least four thousand criminal offenses detailed in the US Code that can be punished under United States law.

"Federal statutory law," Robertson writes, "is set forth under fifty separate headings in the U.S. Code, including everything from arson, robbery, murder, and chemical weapons offenses, to bankruptcy, civil rights abuses, securities fraud, tort law judgments, and dozens more. Title 18 of the code deals with Crimes and Criminal Procedure, but it doesn't contain a complete listing of all the punishable crimes it covers, and it doesn't even define what a crime is."[2]

The fifty titles within the US Code cover more than twenty-seven thousand pages of printed text, and crimes that carry serious criminal penalties are scattered through the other forty-nine titles. To read the judicial interpretations of the legal proceedings involved in all those laws, you would have to slog your way through some twenty-eight hundred volumes and more than four million pages of legal jargon to find all the opinions that have been rendered by judges in those cases.

By comparison, the Ten Commandments is a marvel of simplicity—so simple that a child can commit them all to memory, and many have done exactly that. The greatest problem facing the nation in this election year is not the moral basis of our laws but the risk of putting men and women into high office who would gladly change our laws and customs and who want nothing more than to expand the size and reach of government into every area of our lives.

Whether it's government-funded health care, raising taxes for public education, the environment, alternative fuels, or an alphabet soup of expensive new social programs, there are candidates out there right now who are just dreaming about how they can get government's hands a little deeper into your pockets. Is that what we really want? Or isn't it time to stop, take stock, and look for a better way?

KNOWING WHO YOU ARE

Before deciding where you want to be involved in the political process, you need to think seriously about the issues that motivate you most strongly. Completing a political profile like the one I've described in these pages is a great way to spell it out in black and white. Once you've prioritized your interests based on your concern for your nation, your community, and your children's future, you can begin to apply those standards to the grid set out in chapter 3.

The candidates and their positions should then fall into place. There may not be a perfect candidate, so don't wait for perfection. The fact that no one candidate has captured the public's imagination in the presidential sweepstakes tells us that you may have to settle for the best available option, even if you have to hold your nose to do it. Your first obligation is to maintain your faith and your commitment to Christ as you define it. God the Father is not a demanding or exacting God. The Christian gospel is a very simple message: receive the gift of His Son, by grace through faith, and be obedient to the Holy Spirit's direction. Even a child can do it.

Then, once you've considered your spiritual perspectives and thought carefully about the social and political issues that get your motor running, you need to be prepared to communicate your views to others as you're able. If you can simply do those two things, you will already be light-years ahead of most folks these days. So many of our neighbors will sit around whining and complaining about the situation in Washington, or griping about high taxes or politically correct social policies, and then do absolutely nothing about it. But you don't have to be that way. You have a voice and a vote, and you can make a difference.

Over the years I've had my differences with the media. As you can imagine, running a national campaign for a controversial public figure like Pat Robertson can be a challenge. By and large, the media were fair with me whenever I had news to report or an important press release I wanted to disseminate. But there were some who, no matter how well we did our job, did their dead-level best to silence the message and ignore what Pat had to say. Eventually, I had to learn to keep plugging, regardless of what these naysayers would do. And I found that if I kept a positive spirit and just kept on putting the message out there, even the most liberal pundits would eventually come around and address the message on its merits.

David Broder is a senior political writer for the *Washington Post*. I've encountered David on many occasions in my work, and I've always found him to be respectful of other people's ideas, noncondescending, and professional in his presentation of the facts. He's a journalist in the best sense of the word. There were times when I disagreed with his approach to Pat's campaign. But as the months wore on, I realized the news media weren't the problem. As long as we persisted and just kept putting out the message, the base would do the rest.

Cokie Roberts, who appears on the Sunday news magazine *This Week With George Stephanopoulos*, couldn't be nicer. On more than one occasion, she would stop and ask about my family, how the kids were doing, and how life was treating us.

She's a gifted analyst who gets it right most of the time. The reason that professionals like David and Cokie are so good is that they're not threatened. They're confident in who they are, they know what they believe, and they do not have to destroy anyone else to advance their position. And there's a lesson in that.

There's no reason why you have to be afraid to say what you want to say to your peer group. However, I would agree with something that David Broder wrote in one of his columns: the decline of Western civilization and our cultural slide began with the introduction of the designated hitter rule in the American League. As silly as that may sound, that one bit of equivocation in America's national pastime set a new standard, which said that you can have substitutes and surrogates to cover your weaknesses, so the guy at the plate doesn't have to be accountable. Some people would say that's a bit of a stretch, but I'm not so sure.

To have overreacted and made enemies in the press corps would have been the exact wrong thing for me to do. So, I kept my cool, kept putting the word out, and even though Pat Robertson eventually dropped out of the race, a number of amazing things happened. I've never spoken to Pat about this, but I believe now that it was God's will that Pat Robertson run for the White House. I don't know whether God intended for him to win the election. God's plan is always about the process, not the end result. Rather, I believe He used Pat's campaign to raise up sixty million evangelical voters who, because of their faith, their love for their families, and their deep moral concern for the future of this country, could one day influence the destiny of the nation.

Many of the voters who went to the polls in 1988 had never participated in a political campaign of any kind. Many had never voted for a president. But because of the moral dimensions of the race and the issues Pat Robertson raised, they found their voices, and they decided to get involved. The real miracle is that most of those people are still active today. Pat still has a powerful, world-changing ministry, so he didn't lose very much when he decided to step aside and give his support to George Bush. But just think how God used him to spread the word in that campaign. The emergence of the Christian Right changed everything, and our greatest triumphs are yet to come, and I believe Pat would agree with me on that.

FAITHFUL TO THE CALL

From start to finish, the Robertson campaign was a test of courage and fortitude. There's one more story that Pat related to me that I ought to mention because it shows very well just how tough the pressures could be in that election. On one occasion, Pat and Dede were on their knees praying about the campaign. Pat's prayer was for strength and endurance, for wisdom in debating the issues and compassion for the people he felt led to serve. Like David, constantly pursued by his enemies, he also asked for protection from his adversaries.

Dede's prayer, on the other hand, was simple and to the point. She said, "Lord, give my husband the hide of an elephant." Whenever Pat would tell this story, it always brought laughter from the audience, but it was an appropriate prayer. Our adversaries were relentless, as one incident at the start of the campaign made very clear to all of us.

Pat had chosen the impoverished Bedford-Stuyvesant neighborhood of New York City, where he had lived as a young seminary student many years earlier, as the location from which to kick off his campaign. The street where the announcement took place was a row of brownstones where Pat had begun his career. We got the proper licenses and permits we needed from the City of New York so we could rope off a block of that street. And there was a reviewing stand from which the various speeches would be delivered. The event would be filmed and broadcast later to our supporters around the country.

There was just one problem. The group ACT UP, a militant gay/lesbian organization, was protesting Pat's campaign and his presence in that city. This is the same group that barricaded itself in churches and chained themselves to the pews in St. Patrick's Cathedral, railing against any church that didn't recognize and applaud the gay and lesbian lifestyle. They turned up in large numbers at Pat's campaign rally. They indicated that they were going to charge the barricades like a band of vigilantes, but the New York police surrounded the area to prevent them from reaching the reviewing stand.

Some of these men had vials of bodily fluids in their hands, holding them over their heads and shaking them, threatening to throw AIDS-tainted blood and urine on the crowd. They shouted at the top of their lungs so that nobody from the platform could be heard. When I saw what was happening, I realized we couldn't allow this rabble to disrupt what we had planned. So I told each of the participants, including Pat, to go ahead and give their speeches as if the protesters weren't there, even though there was a good chance the speakers couldn't be heard beyond the first few rows.

At that point I discussed the situation with the police sergeant in charge of the location. He told me there was nothing he could do about their presence, their vocal outbursts, or their blatant disrespect for our freedom of speech. But he said that if they crossed the barricades, as they were threatening to do, he would arrest them and secure the perimeter. I don't know what the officers said to the ACT UP crowd, but I could see that the protestors weren't going to challenge New York's finest.

So we went ahead with the announcement as if we were talking to our friends all across the United States. Pat's announcement speech and each of the others, by the various notables we had invited, had been printed and handed out to the press in advance. Even with all the racket behind us, the journalists covering the event would be able to follow what was being said from the printed text.

The next day, every newspaper and broadcast outlet that covered the event condemned ACT UP for not giving Pat the right to speak freely. Pictures of the protestors, dressed and painted like savages and waving their vulgar signs and images, were circulated around the world. Even by today's standards, those images were shocking. As a result, Christians all over the country rallied to our support, and public endorsements and financial support poured in to the campaign. Because of that demonstration, which was meant to desecrate the event, we got much better response to Pat's announcement than we might have if there had there been no protestors at all.

Because of Pat's determination to say what he had come to say, and because he and the team demonstrated no fear of their adversaries, the base rallied, and that was an important lesson for all of us. We found that if we showed leadership and courage to advocate for what we knew to be right, that would encourage everyone who understood our objectives and cared about our issues to join ranks. And in the face of what may appear to be insurmountable odds, positive gains can still be made. The key is being faithful to the call and standing on principle.

RUNNING ON PRINCIPLE

Not all candidates find themselves in those circumstances, and not all candidates are the same. There's no single method for finding the right person to run for office, and the best person for the job may not always be so easy to spot. In that regard, I think the example of Eldon Rudd is a good one. Eldon was a tall, lanky, folksy type of guy. He reminded me of Abe Lincoln by his demeanor and posture. He was a man of substance with good ideas, but he always exhibited genuine humility and was cordial with everyone he met.

When Eldon decided to run for Congress in 1976, the odds were stacked against him. His home district was in far-eastern Arizona, on the New Mexico border, which was a heavily Democratic working-class district. It resembled a district that had once been served by Morris "Mo" Udall. To get anywhere in the campaign, Eldon would have to restructure the grass roots, as I've described in previous chapters. But there didn't appear to be a way in the world he could do that, and no way could he win the race. There were barely enough Republicans in the district to get a decent endorsement. Democrats had controlled it for years, and the labor unions had pledged to keep that district in the liberal camp.

What no one had counted on, however, was that the grass roots in eastern Arizona was made up of individuals who were deeply concerned about the direction of the country, and they were determined to work for Eldon if for no other reason than the fact that they felt it was the right thing to do. The Committee for the Survival of a Free Congress, headed by Paul Weyrich, had identified this race as one in which the various grassroots organization could actually make a difference. Paul had been working with a new system called the Kasten Plan, which was a concept for precinct organization in areas with a highly mixed electorate, and he asked me to help put that concept to work.

The author of the Kasten Plan was a businessman from Racine, Wisconsin, named Fritz Rench. He developed the plan as a volunteer for then Senator Bob Kasten of Wisconsin. What he had done was outline a strategy for getting the grass roots involved, giving people specific directions on how to organize and get out the vote so they could make their goal projections. During Eldon's congressional race, Paul and others decided this was the perfect place to see if the Kasten Plan would really work, and we got busy to make it happen. The vote goal process was merged with some of our other coalition-building operations, bringing people into the campaign by issues and helping them organize by precinct.

With just three weeks left in the campaign, the numbers showed that Eldon Rudd was behind his Democratic opponent by more than twelve percentage points. But Eldon's people weren't discouraged by that. They believed in what they were doing and they just kept pushing ahead because, again, it was the right thing to do. They organized by precinct, applying coalition politics by issue, and their efforts paid off.

By sheer dedication and hard work, they reached the vote goals they needed to establish the viability of their candidate, and by sheer force of will and unity of purpose, Eldon Rudd won an upset victory. But what I like about this story most of all is that it's such a great object lesson for us today. In the face of long odds and obstacles that may often seem insurmountable, such as working against the media and many other forces over which we have no control, there's still hope for turning things around and winning the race. Sometimes it means working a little harder. But sometimes it's just a matter of keeping the faith and running on principle.

FINDING YOUR VOICE

We have a lot more ways to get the word out these days with conservative talk shows and conservative news outlets, but in some ways that really doesn't matter anymore, because now there's a base of conservative values voters who have taken ownership of the issues. These conservative voters aren't stupid. They know what they want. They have courage and strong convictions, and by God's grace I believe they're more passionate today than ever before.

The liberal media may try to ignore us, and they may even slow us down. But ultimately they can't stop us. If the national press had all the influence that some of them think they have, Ronald Reagan would never have been nominated, let alone elected president. The editorials against him in both of his presidential campaigns were beyond brutal; they were savage. Some of the editorial writers called him a madman. "He's going to get us into a nuclear war with Russia" was the mantra from the Left at the time, and the Democrats really made an issue of it. But the Christian Right and the conservative New Right rejected those attacks and worked even harder.

I found the national press to be liberal but not oppressive and certainly not censoring. They may not have agreed with me on very many things; they may have thought I was off the mark on most of them; but they printed what I said. Also, for the most part I found them to be normal people with the same emotions and same concern for the future that we have. Most of the reporters and pundits I've worked with are decent people.

Ronald Reagan had made it socially acceptable for us to be conservatives. Pat put the face on the Christian Right. Reagan changed the debate over whether or not limited government and free enterprise should be part of the national conversation. Pat Robertson made it socially acceptable to be a Christian conservative. To make its mark on the culture, every movement must have a credible candidate in the race for president. Pat Robertson served that role for the Christian activist. At great personal sacrifice, he mainstreamed Christians into politics. Never again can anyone allege that the number of Christian conservatives in this country—who have a personal relationship with Christ, and who are willing to defend their faith to the death—is less than 5 percent of the population.

There's one other thing you should know about Pat Robertson. At his core, he is the real deal. Yes, he occasionally says different things, and sometimes he seems a bit unorthodox.

I can also tell you he was hard to work for at times. I worked side by side with him in times of crisis, and I observed his commitment to his faith when no one else was watching, and he never disappointed me. But to make the point, maybe a story from the campaign trail would be in order.

During the heat of the campaign, Pat was asked to make a major address to a joint session of the New Hampshire state legislature. The speech had been billed as a major policy presentation of the campaign; one way or the other, this address would define the differences between our campaign and all the others. We were overly ambitious in our timing and had put a lot of pressure on the staff back in Virginia Beach to get us a final draft of Pat's speech on time. There was no e-mail in those days, only fax machines. On top of that, the weather was bitterly cold and snowing.

For whatever reason, we never got Pat's copy of the speech. We were waiting anxiously in a holding room just outside the House Speaker's platform. There must have been one hundred fifty reporters and photographers from all over the country in the room. The chamber was packed. But there we were with no speech and no notes for Pat to work from. We waited as long as we could until the sergeant at arms called us to the podium. That cleared the waiting room so that the only people left were a security guard, Pat, and me.

They say you know a man by what he does when no one else is watching. This was one of those times. Pat was disappointed, but he didn't lose his temper. He didn't panic. He dropped to his knees and prayed for counsel from Jesus. That was it. When he stood up, he entered the House chamber, went up to the podium, and gave the best speech he could without notes of any kind. Throughout the campaign, he was always what he appeared to be: a man of God.

Regardless of what anyone may say about the Christian Right today, they found their voice in that race and built a platform for the future. As the gavel of leadership passes now to a new generation of younger, born-again leaders, we ought to be doing everything we can to help them succeed in the process of deciding who, how, and what philosophy they will support in the coming forty-year cycle. Not every election will be a landslide, and not every candidate will be a Ronald Reagan. There are times when we may have to settle for our second choice, but the decision to find our voices and get involved is not an option. We have to do it.

THE LOOK OF A LEADER

President George W. Bush, more than any other president in my lifetime, has been respectful and sensitive to Christian concerns. He has a way of keeping his priorities straight. No one knows how history will treat his presidency, but he's not the problem, and he's not the public menace he's made out to be by the liberal media and their friends on the far Left. He has kept the factions of the conservative movement in balance by not giving preferential treatment to any of them. Any anger at President Bush among conservatives today, in my opinion, is based more on the general atmosphere of discontent at this time than anything else. People are frustrated, concerned, disappointed, but they haven't changed their values.

At the end of the presidential primary process in 1988, the Republican Party sponsored a series of unity dinners to unite the base around the nominee, President Bush's father, George H. W. Bush (whom I refer to as Bush 41). George W. was the owner and managing partner of the Texas Rangers Baseball Club at that time. I had the opportunity to travel with him to a couple of those dinners and introduce some of the local state leaders to the Bush 41 campaign team. Businessman George W. couldn't have been nicer, in public or private, or more gracious in receiving our support.

At the 1996 Republican National Convention in San Diego, Bill Greener was the convention manager, and I was on board as part of his team. One evening I was manning the post under the well of the speaker's podium. It was my job to keep things moving on schedule, solving problems on the spot. George W. Bush, then governor of Texas, was addressing the National Convention. In the well, waiting for their turn at the microphone, were two senators and two congressmen whom I will not name. They were arguing about who should go next and who would get the best time slot.

At 6:00 p.m. Pacific time, it would be 9:00 p.m. in New York, which would be prime time for the television audience. The sweet spot to be seen on nationwide television was between 6:00 and 7:00 p.m. in San Diego, which would be 9:00 to 10:00 p.m. on the East Coast and 8:00 to 9:00 p.m. in the Central time zone. It was still just 5:00 p.m. where we were, and each speaker would have thirty minutes to make their remarks. This meant that two of them would have to go on before prime time and two after. As they jockeyed back and forth to see who would get the best time slot, the argument became heated.

The four officials turned to me for a solution, but I had a schedule to keep that had been given to me by the convention manager, and I intended to enforce it. Each of the elected officials gave me all the reasons why they should be repositioned on the schedule, and when I explained my position, they tried to argue that someone else had suggested the schedule could be changed. Two of the speakers were just fine with the schedule, but the other two were acting more like kids fighting over a piece of candy.

A STICKY SITUATION

I wasn't about to call Bill Greener and tell him that I couldn't handle the situation. And I wasn't about to go to Haley Barbour, who was the Republican National Committee chairman at the time. When I realized that these guys weren't going to leave me alone, I said, "Gentlemen, the chairman of the convention will be coming off the podium in fifteen seconds. You can appeal your case to him, if you like." When then governor George W. Bush descended from the podium to the well, I quickly briefed him on the situation and told him that I intended to enforce the schedule I'd been given.

All four of those politicians surrounded Bush trying to get his attention, all at the same time. They had less than three minutes to plead their case before one of them would have to go up to the podium and give his speech. So George W. thought about it for a second, then said, "Do you fellows have your season tickets to Rangers baseball?" They were befuddled. Baseball? Mr. Bush continued, "Well, then, you're going to miss a heck of a baseball season."

At that point he looked around at me and asked, "Who's the next speaker, Marc?" I told him what was on the schedule and he grabbed my arm and took me with him, leaving those guys to execute the schedule as it had been designed. I can tell you, I appreciated the rescue, but I was really impressed with the way George Bush handled that situation. He was never one to become unnerved or be too impressed with titles. He treated everyone equally.

The need for a coalition of social conservatives, Christian conservatives, economic conservatives, foreign policy conservatives, and government conservatives to work together is greater today than ever before. When we have a common central purpose that's consistent with each of our specific concerns, the coalition will be stronger than the individual members could ever be by themselves. To make the point, maybe I can use a baseball analogy.

In the late 1980s, I attended an early-season game at Fenway Park in Boston. I was sitting in the right-field bleachers. It was cold that night, but the stadium was packed. The Red Sox were playing the Angels, and the faithful were all there. As I looked around, I couldn't help but notice the diversity of everyone around me: there were guys in coats and ties, and some in parkas and ties. There were blue-collar workers, African Americans, whites, and Hispanics—men and women of every description.

At one point I asked the guy next to me what he did for a living. He said he was an accountant. The guy in front of us was an electrician. They had sat in the same seats for years, and they knew each other very well. In about the third inning, I noticed that people were looking back at the scoreboard and booing. The Red Sox were ahead, so I didn't understand why they would be booing. When I asked the accountant what was going on, he said they hadn't updated the batting averages for the first two games. I had to laugh. These guys weren't just keeping the box score, they were keeping the batting averages as well.

As it turned out, the electrician had already done most of the calculations before the game. The accountant had a sophisticated calculator in his pocket. Before long there were about nine rows of people feeding information to the electrician's database, while the accountant was punching out the numbers and updating the averages. Now, that was a bunch of people from diverse backgrounds all working together for a common cause. It was a perfect illustration of the kind of cooperation that can make such a big difference in the political arena when people are motivated to get involved.

As an aside, one of the Angels made a legitimate steal of home from third base. That was the first and last time I've ever seen that happen. I would have expected the Boston fans to be upset with the guy, since it gave the other team the lead. But, instead, the Red Sox fans gave the runner a standing ovation and called him back out of the visitors' dugout for a bow. Now that's dedication to the game, and another illustration of the temperament of a winning coalition.

I'm convinced that the success of any coalition depends on the commitment of the individuals involved. Shallow issues don't hold a crowd; strong coalitions only come together around the big questions and in stressful times. This is something my mentor, Milton Friedman, has said on many occasions. True and lasting change only comes in times of crisis, and there's no question that we're at that point today, as so many alien forces are at work, here and around the world, attempting to weaken our resolve. We will need godly wisdom and strong leadership to overcome that challenge.

HONESTY AND TRANSPARENCY

The candidacy of Governor Mike Huckabee has surprised many pundits, to say the least. He has built a steady and growing following by his honesty and his appeal to the common man. He speaks from the heart and appears to most people to be genuine. There's a quote on exhibit at the Saint Sophia Cathedral Museum in Istanbul, Turkey, in what was once the Roman emperor Constantine's official Christian church. The admonition is, "Appear to be what you are or be what you appear to be." I believe Governor Huckabee lives by this creed. He cares for the working man and his plight in today's changing world. Honesty and transparency is what the new leadership of the Christian movement has been asking for. Could such a man be the bridge between the old and new conservative movements in the United States?

Our challenge in the upcoming election will be to probe the issues well enough to learn the values of the candidates and examine their record of achievement to determine who really has the capacity to lead this nation for the next four or eight years. Each of the current and former front-runners in this race has qualities to be admired, whether it's serving in Congress, being a war hero, managing several billion-dollar corporations and the U.S. Olympic Committee, serving as the mayor of a major city, or being the governor of a Southern state. The credentials matter, but we must also think about the intangibles, from personality and leadership skills to their religious beliefs and record of support for individual liberty and limited government. It's not an easy task, but this is the remarkable privilege the founders of our nation purchased for us with their own blood.

I think it's important to say something about where we stand on the diplomatic front at this juncture since current events and turmoil around the world always seem to keep these issues in front of us. I had the pleasure of working with the late Benazir Bhutto of Pakistan, and I spoke with her once about the development of democracy in her country. I was part of a team that advised the former prime minister on the application of free enterprise. My assignment was to brief her on speaking engagements in the United States on how to relate her topics to an American audience. I told her that to achieve true free enterprise, the government must be open, fair, and accountable to the people. However, it is precisely this transparency, as I warned her, that gives so many totalitarian governments so much grief.

This became especially clear to me on one of my missions to the Middle East. In February of 2004, I participated in a project to advise the mayors of several towns in Jordan about municipal finance. The purpose of the project was to help the mayors determine revenue streams they could generate at the local level for use in their cities. Every government action in Jordan involving money is a federal initiative. It became apparent to me in interviewing these men and one woman that they weren't as concerned about democracy as they were about accountability. The Arab League sponsored a regional conference in Amman to address the topic of development within their member states, and I was invited to attend. What the members proposed was that Western governments stress democracy less and its attributes more.

In other words, they were saying, "We may have problems in our part of the world with American-style democracy, but we would still like to know the goals and results that democratic countries should produce. If you would tell us more about the five principles of democracy—the rule of law, transparency in government, the value of a free press, bureaucratic accountability, and free trade—perhaps we can find some aspects of democracy on which our governments will agree."

Hearing those comments made me realize that if the United States government would advocate Americanism as its principal export rather than a view of democracy that says "one size fits all," our democratic values might get a more receptive hearing. One of the main purposes of the five points of democracy listed above—which I had shared with these Jordanian leaders—is to eliminate corruption. No one can legitimately support corruption in government. It's only when corruption is curtailed that freedom can be pursued.

I happen to believe that, had she lived and regained her seat as Pakistan's leader, Benazir Bhutto's open and free enterprise economic platform would have achieved all of the above goals. And beyond that, the movement she was leading could have been part of a worldwide movement to eliminate corruption. Those in power who use corrupt tactics to advance their own interests will of course fight such reforms, and that is what no doubt led to Mrs. Bhutto's tragic death. But I would also say that it's very difficult to hide behind rhetoric that attempts to obscure this reality. No one can run from the truth forever.

TOWARD A UNITED FRONT

In his book *A House Divided*, Mark Gerzon, who is a specialist in conflict resolution, has written that people who care deeply for democracy are committed to making it succeed. But he also says that there are a half dozen different political perspectives, or worldviews, competing for allegiance in America today. These six forces, or states, he says, are struggling for America's soul, which leads to divisions and conflict on many fronts.[3]

Gerzon identifies the six as the religious state, the capitalist state, the disempowered state, the superstate, the transformation state, and the governing state. He gives them classical Greek names and says that the objective of each state ought to be better understanding and cooperation between all these diverse interests, leading to a "new patriotism" fueled by unity of purpose. When the book first appeared in 1996, it caused quite a stir in political circles. Many of the terms and ideas Gerzon used seemed to apply to the situation in Washington during the Clinton years, when there was so much division and hostility.

In one section of the book, titled "Practicing the New Patriotism," he suggests that the American people need to join a campaign. Not a Republican or Democratic campaign, but an American campaign; not a campaign for public office, but a campaign for our country. At the heart of his argument, he says, is a concern that we're in danger of losing the principles of good citizenship, and I think that's a legitimate concern.

There are ideas in the book that are controversial. Gerzon's interest in conflict resolution, unfortunately, causes him to question the importance of defending our national interests when we're threatened by men and nations whose ideas are radically different from our own. But his thoughts on forming a coalition and working across disciplines to achieve our common aims are excellent. They make a lot of sense because that's the position we're in today. As Christians and conservatives of many backgrounds and perspectives, we have an opportunity to set in motion a dynamic new movement of individuals united by our love for this country.

My friend David Boren, who is president of University of

Oklahoma and a former United States senator and Oklahoma governor, once said to me, "Believe in something bigger than yourself, then pursue it with passion." I took those words to heart, and that's all I'm really saying to you in these pages. You and I believe in something bigger than ourselves, and we also believe in someone who is greater than all the troubles we've been asked to endure. As the apostle John assures us, "He who is in you is greater than he who is in the world" (1 John 4:4). And our cause, to restore the dignity and greatness of this great land, is a challenge worthy of a great and resourceful people.

In his new book, *A Letter to America*, Dr. Boren argues that we must find bipartisan solutions to America's pressing problems, and I know that's something many people would agree with.[4]

Not all unity is good, of course. I can think of a dozen examples of unified, passionate, well-funded coalitions that are dangerous to America's future and that need to be resisted—there's not a lot of room for compromise when it comes to the sanctity of life, same-sex marriage, church and state issues, the war on terrorism and the security of Israel, and the like. But to have any chance of winning those debates, achieving victory at the polls, and truly changing the focus of the nation, we will need a united front, led by men and women we can trust.

As we turn a corner now to take a look at some of the challenges beyond our shores, we ought to pause to remember where we've come from and where we need to go from here. Forty years ago, the seeds of a dynamic new coalition were planted by a visionary leader who had no idea that one day he would be remembered as the greatest president of our generation. At this hour, we still don't know which way the nation will turn on election day. Either we will take the first step backward toward a thousand years of darkness, or we will turn the corner toward the destiny we've been hoping and praying for for years. One of those two visions will become a reality. But which will it be?

Chapter 5

FOR THE COMMON GOOD

Whenever you do a thing, though it can never be known but to yourself, ask yourself how you would act were all the world looking at you, and act accordingly.[1]

—THOMAS JEFFERSON

The Bible says two things that relate to politics. First, don't worry. Second, take each day one day at a time. When the Israelites were wandering in the desert, manna came down from heaven every morning. It couldn't be stored or collected for more than a day. The Israelites had to trust that the Lord would give them everything they needed for that day. We may have more options today, particularly in the food department, but we need to do the same, trusting that God will provide for our needs each day. It's part of the request in the Lord's Prayer, "Give us this day our daily bread." It doesn't just mean food or spiritual nourishment, but *all you need*.

In order to deal with all the complicated questions before us these days and to know our positions on the issues, we may need to simplify the process. Whether or not you choose to apply what my associates call the "Nuttle Grid" in chapter 3, you can use the same basic formula as an outline to develop your own structure. The first thing you need to do is to determine what you believe as universal principles. For example, most of us would never look to government for all our needs or depend on the state to take care of us. Wherever you place your faith and trust is where you worship. You don't want government to be your god. Therefore, you must never place yourself or your family in the position of being totally dependent on anything other than God.

In the future, all decisions about government programs and solutions ought to be based on whether or not we believe that deciding in favor of some new proposal will make government more accountable to us or make us more accountable to government. Whether the issue is economic development or crime prevention, environmental policy or poverty, health care or social security, foreign affairs or states' rights, determining whether or not we support a proposed activity should be based of whether or not it would tend to enslave us.

When I was consulting for the National Federation of Independent Business (NFIB) in the early 1990s, I was working on a television program for small business. We had approached a major technological firm with the prospect of not only sponsoring the program but also helping to design an interactive component of the information to be disseminated to the public. This was at a time when no one completely understood the depth and reach of the Internet, but everyone could see it coming.

The corporate leader I spoke to said he thought his organization could build and control a global data network. In other words, they wanted to own and operate the Internet. But what they actually found out the hard way was the lesson that free enterprise and freedom of opportunity continue to teach us, which is that any system that allows people to act freely and without restriction will allow individuals to come up with innovative solutions that will outstrip and outperform a managed system every time.

As the executives of that company began seeing what was actually happening with the World Wide Web, they realized how foolish they had been, and confessed that they were embarrassed they had ever considered the possibility of controlling the Internet. At one point they had asked our delegation from the NFIB to sign a nondisclosure agreement saying that anything we learned at their headquarters was protected intellectual property. They were afraid we might give away some of their closely guarded secrets. But they discovered that they needed to go back to the drawing board and think about what they could actually accomplish. They let themselves get carried away, but this time they were determined to take a more practical approach.

THE DYNAMICS OF FREEDOM

I report all this not to criticize the naïveté of the organization but to point out that this happened before the Internet had become what it is today. For some reason I wasn't asked to sign their nondisclosure agreement. But at the end of the first day's meetings, a young software engineer approached me from nowhere. I hadn't seen him in the meetings and I didn't see him afterward. But he singled me out and asked if I was Marc Nuttle. I said I was, and then he asked if I was, in fact, the member of the delegation who was familiar with the inner workings of government, and particularly with the relationship between public policy and public opinion.

Needless to say I was a little surprised by his level of specificity, but I confessed I was guilty as charged. The young man seemed very serious about talking to me directly, so I told him I would be curious to hear his comments or questions, whatever they might be. Now, I'm usually cautious when a stranger approaches me in that manner with such a definitive agenda, but by this point I was curious to see what this young fellow had on his mind.

He said, "Mr. Nuttle, there's one thing you must understand about the Internet. You can't control it. You either have to totally release it and let matters fall where they may, or you have to control individuals and restrict how it's used. That will result in controlling people, but it will not control the Internet."

As you can imagine, I was taken aback by these unsolicited comments coming at me from out of the blue. But I was intrigued. This was obviously a bright young man who had looked into the future and thought about the ramifications of creating a global data network, so I stepped aside with him to hear what else he had to say. I realized he was telling me the truth, but he was also giving me some kind of warning.

We spoke for several minutes about the challenges the Internet would bring, providing instant access to a previously unimaginable range of information, all potentially within the reach of every home and office on the planet. It would mean an explosion of new facts and data, but it would also be the biggest challenge to freedom and dignity the world has ever seen. After he had stated his views and convinced me this was worth further study, he said he wanted to ask me about something of vital importance.

His question was: "What will Congress do, and what will the American public accept, when they realize that their freedom depends upon a totally open and free Internet with all the positive benefits as well as the mischief that could mean?" Total freedom means that people with bad intentions will have the same access to information and the same means of reaching out and touching someone. The only way to limit that sort of access would be to license everyone on the Web and legislate criminal sanctions for anyone who attempts to access the network without a license. The price of security is total govern-ment control, but is that what we want?

The second part of his question was, "What do you think will happen to this country if we agree to that type of tracking system for our everyday communications? And what will happen if the rest of the world refuses to follow suit? In either case we will still be threatened by organized crime." After posing his question, the young engineer looked at me intently and said, "Mr. Nuttle, that is the real question we need to ask. Are the American people ready for the challenges the Internet will pose to our future? And do you think the people in Washington will be able to leave well enough alone?"

AN UNEXPECTED RISK

It took a while for me to process everything the young man was saying, but as I reflected on his comments later, I began to see what he meant. The communications capacity of the World Wide Web will be so vast and so diverse in form that virtually anything that can be known will be available online. Students will be able to do their homework online, researching original documents and gathering information from literally millions of sources in no time at all. On the other hand, criminals and spies and others with much less honorable intentions can access personal records and information they have no business seeing. And that's the dilemma.

Either we turn it all loose and encourage people to protect themselves as best they can through software filters, fire-walls, and careful storage of their sensitive information, or we find some way to grant licenses with numbered registration codes to make sure that nothing can be stolen or transferred electronically without certain knowledge that the authorities will be able to track all that information on the Internet and apprehend whoever generated it. Either we give people total freedom or we take that freedom away. These are the only two options.

Unlicensed activity on the Internet would have to be regulated like illegal drugs. If you're caught with drugs, you're guilty—it's called illegal possession. It's very difficult to defend against a charge of illegal possession unless you can prove that somebody slipped the drugs into your backpack without your knowledge. A license to use the Internet tied to a fingerprint, a DNA sample, a retinal scan, or something of that nature would make it very difficult for someone else to be on the Internet and associate the activity with you unless you were actually involved. But do we want security measures to be that invasive?

If government wants to control organized crime or illegal gambling or to have access to information discussed between different members of an underground terrorist network, they will either need unrestricted privileges to snoop on private citizens, or every citizen who uses the Internet will have to be licensed in some way so that everything they do can be traced back to them. The young engineer went on to say that even if you could control it inside the United States, that would be pointless if other nations didn't enforce the same laws. All you would have to do if you wanted to break the law would be to travel to some other country and use the Internet from a safe distance.

At the time of this encounter, terrorism was not yet a priority issue for the United States. But the questions I was asked, and the conversation with that young engineer, take on a new importance today in light of this new threat. What he was concerned about was organized crime laundering money through offshore entities that could corrupt and destroy our economy. Unchecked and unrestricted access to the Internet would allow members of organized crime and drug dealers to operate in such a way that they could not be detected, and people intent on pilfering personal information off the Web could continue to infiltrate our society.

We know more about these concerns today, and the kinds of filters, locks, and firewalls he described are now available. But there are still many important questions and problems that need to be addressed. The political questions haven't been answered. There have been several attempts by Congress and the United Nations to regulate the Web. The liberal politicians who scream loudest about invasion of privacy have been eager to make the Internet a pay-for-play option, closely regulated and monitored by the state. But any government that controls and licenses communications between citizens is a government that can decide for itself what it wants to outlaw and what it wants to ignore.

WEATHERING THE STORMS

We've talked about the issues facing the country today, including issues that are being debated by the candidates in this year's elections. We've also touched on how the development of new systems and technologies can raise the specter of government control and the invasion of privacy. Once again, this brings us back to a discussion of the proper role of government and the level of freedom we're willing to sacrifice for a certain measure of security.

If you've worked your way through the grid and determined your positions and priorities, the next step is to test those conclusions against your opinions concerning government's role in your life, because there are issues developing at this hour for which you must be prepared, and you may need to be prepared to lead your own peer group if these pressures continue to mount.

A number of prominent economic analysts have predicted recession in 2008. It is upon us. As their voices grow louder, their predictions have become more and more sinister and have the potential of becoming self-fulfilling. There's a difference of opinion about how serious such a recession will be. Time will tell. But how would you react to a worst-case scenario? A very serious recession would mean higher unemployment, less capital investment, retraction in the manufacturing sector, and a tightening of credit controls. None of this may happen, of course, but the prospect of a major financial adjustment is certainly an issue with long-term political implications. What would that mean for you and your family?

My purpose is not to get into an academic discussion of the economic consequences of an event of this type. There are more than a few books dealing with the contrasting views of Milton Friedman and John Kenneth Galbraith on the subject. My point is to suggest that any decision you make regarding your core values and how you intend to express them in the political arena will need to take into account where you place a major economic crisis on your grid and how you measure your responses there against your overriding beliefs about the balance between government control and personal freedom.

Another concern in this election year is fuel prices. Over the past year, gasoline prices in the United States have averaged between $2.50 and $3.50 per gallon for regular unleaded gasoline. For many years economists have believed that gasoline prices were inelastic, meaning that demand does not decrease just because prices increase. You have to drive your car, no matter what the price of gas may be. In 2007, the public proved that there is some elasticity in fuel prices, after all. Demand decreased slightly when prices went above $3.00 per gallon.

The problem is that the price per gallon is a very complicated formula encompassing many world factors. This includes the demand for crude oil in China and other developing parts of the world, increased air traffic and demand for jet fuel, demand for heating fuel and other such needs, and even the impact of weather-related phenomena and infrastructure issues.

Production and refining capacity are key factors in determining the price per gallon.

As gasoline prices increase, various sectors of the economy will be impacted at different rates on a sliding scale of inelasticity. Construction workers cannot drive round-trip more than thirty miles to a job site at current wages in the Midwest when the price per gallon is greater than four dollars. It's not just a matter of being able to afford the fuel; based on average wages for blue-collar workers in that industry, they can't afford the cost increase. This inability to afford fuel on the price-per-gallon basis moves up the wage scale to include higher income workers and commuters from the suburbs when the price reaches five to six dollars per gallon.

But this is where the innovation of the consumer kicks in. As the price of fuel goes up, innovation occurs. People will carpool. Some white-collar workers may only come into the office two or three days a week. Some industries will adjust to the changes quicker than others, but some individuals will change jobs. On the other hand, incomes may go up to cover the cost. Then again, prices may stabilize or begin to decline.

It would appear that if there is a mild recession and the world's demand for goods and services continues to increase, the demand for oil will go up faster than suppliers can provide. If the price goes down, it may be because there's less demand. And, here again, less demand may be driven by innovation, or conservation, or because the recession has changed the entire equation.

Regardless of the issues that may arise now or later, many people will demand government solutions. Certainly those within the liberal camp who have adapted to a worldview in which government is the great benefactor of mankind will be the first to demand intervention from Washington. They may want direct subsidies, tax breaks, investment incentives, or other types of assistance, in which case you ought to be prepared to think about these things in a reasonable manner based on your hopes for your children's future and what you believe about the inherent risks of centralized control and managed economies.

THE NEED FOR CITIZEN LEADERS

The Christian Right, as I've said in previous chapters, sought changes in government to impact the culture and preserve essential moral values. Some of the younger generation within the movement today are more concerned with social ills such as poverty, AIDS, the environment, chronic diseases, and education. If these folks want to make a lasting impact in those areas of concern, they will have to establish programs that offer the kinds of services they propose, along with systems to measure their results. The standard of proof is high for such groups. Programs big enough to change behaviors and deal with social problems will need to be established and recognized by government. They must be capable of providing needed services that can be measured in social and economic terms, and they must show proof of positive results.

President George W. Bush, with input from scholars such as Marvin Olasky and John DiIulio, established the government's program of federally funded faith-based initiatives. They put the systems in place and began a massive public relations campaign, but the results were not measurable and were attacked by the media and the Democratic Party for being inconsequential and unreliable. Faith-based organizations could submit proposals for government funding. Such funding was often based on projected expenses but not measured in the total cost to address the problems that the organization originally set out to correct. So, in many cases there were serious shortfalls in revenue and accusations of the misapplication of funds.

There's no question that citizen involvement in these kinds of public service projects is a good idea, and systems to facilitate and fund charitable causes are much needed. In the Northeast, the Catholic church has long taken an active role in providing schools, hospitals, and welfare and relief services, as well as higher education opportunities in partnership with the states and local communities. The services the Catholic church provides are funded primarily by charitable contributions and money provided by the denomination. To the extent these services supplement existing taxpayer-funded initiatives, they can reduce the amount of government funding that is needed while avoiding direct government control and interference.

But how can the Christian community provide similar types of assistance in other places? Needs-based medical care is an idea that has been around for a long time but which nobody wants to talk about. If you earn enough to be able to pay for private medical care, then an option for you might be to forgo Medicare, or to participate in a reduced-scale program. This would be optional, of course. But every person who does this would be making a measurable impact on the system. Every dollar of assistance you forgo would reduce the pressures on the system when fewer workers are paying into the Social Security fund and the baby-boom generation is suddenly reaching retirement age.

Another idea that has not been widely discussed but that I believe could make a tremendous contribution is the idea that every American give two years of service to their country. If you serve in the military, that would count as your contribution. No one could ask for more than that. Otherwise, there could be programs to engage private citizens in helping out in some aspect of government or public service in accordance with their skills, interests, or occupation. It might be that you could serve as an accountant for the city for a period of time, or as an administrator for the county. There would need to be a service infrastructure through which each volunteer could contribute a certain number of hours each week, but this could be a benefit for the community and a way for citizens to learn about the inner workings of government.

The system wouldn't work without some sort of recognized program for involving volunteers, but a well-designed program of this type in each community could have a tremendous impact in savings to the community, reducing the cost of government and tax reductions as well. I'm sure there are some who will say that such a system is naïve, that any costs for volunteer assistance in the organizational budget would require a full-time position staffed by a career employee. But that's not necessarily so. That may be the way it's done today, but with a little creative thinking, the system could be restructured to prepare for tomorrow's needs.

A FOUNDATIONAL APPROACH

Another way to serve would be to forgo retirement and all retirement benefits for two years past your current eligibility. This would be dependent upon your ability to do so, physically and financially. Some won't be able to do that but may still be able to volunteer in another capacity. With the right kind of organization and planning, an emerging conservative Christian movement could develop a charitable fund or tax-exempt foundation to help compensate volunteers and reduce the strain on government.

Such a partnership would offer a balanced approach between government's requirement to provide everything and the willingness of individuals to take responsibility for their own needs and services. It would not violate the doctrine of separation of church and state. The state wouldn't need to limit the volunteer program to religious organizations. It would be a service opportunity for any organized group that wants to contribute to the government in a way that saves money and helps to solve problems. But qualified leaders will have to help point the way.

Our primary duty as Christians revolves around our commitment to trust God, obey His commandments, and live each day one day at a time. If we're able, we can also minister and provide useful services to our brothers and sisters, knowing that we will be providing something valuable in this world but that even better rewards may come in the next. There's great comfort in keeping the Great Commandment of loving the Lord with all your heart, mind, soul, and strength, and loving your neighbor as yourself. But doing unto others as we would have them do unto us is not just the Golden Rule; it's a golden opportunity to serve. Remember, you cannot delegate love; you must do it yourself.

Faith doesn't force us to love our neighbors, and that's probably a good thing! But if we're filled with the Holy Spirit, our faith makes us want to love others. When the Spirit of Christ enters your heart, you're thrilled to know you're forgiven and have the free gift of eternal life. You naturally want to do things to help others. But, as I've touched on in previous chapters, free enterprise adds another dimension that says, if I build a paved road today, not only does that help my neighbor, but it also helps me get my goods to market, rain or shine. So the spirit of Christianity and the spirit of free enterprise work together, hand in hand, doing things that are beneficial for the community.

Take away either component, and you don't have the same environment. You may get someone who will take care of his own place but he's not really concerned about how well his neighbors are doing. He may treat you well when you come to his home, but you may not get that same spirit of cooperation unless there's both an economic incentive and a Christian motivation to care about the welfare of your neighbors.

Some people argue that free enterprise leaves too many people behind. If you just turn it loose, those with better opportunities, more talent, or greater wealth will prevail while others will simply fall behind. But in the kind of society I'm describing, that's not going to happen. If there's a deficit of either of these two concerns—the motivation to love God and the incentive to love your neighbors—a spirit of selfishness may appear. But there has to be balance. Our concern for others doesn't have to go to extremes, but nothing does more for the well-being of the community and the nation than working for the common good.

SELF-INTEREST PROPERLY UNDERSTOOD

I occasionally talked to Milton Friedman about spiritual issues, and a couple of times we got into the issue of tithing. He told me that if you run the numbers in a computer model, 10 percent is about right. Roughly 10 percent of the population at any given time needs assistance. And the percent of the people's resources that government ought to be spending for public aid calculates out to around 10 percent. "It's amazing how that works out, isn't it?" he said. "Since you, as a Christian, believe that tithing is a biblical requirement, and we both believe in free enterprise, then maybe the balance is somewhere around the 10 percent number."

Dr. Friedman believed that the worst thing you can do to a man is enslave him so he has to go to the government for his needs every day. The old parable that says, "If you give a man a fish, he eats for a day, but if you teach him to fish, he eats for a lifetime," is really true. But Dr. Friedman said you can ruin a man, even if he learns to fish, if you constantly offer him free food and don't require him to earn it by the sweat of his brow. We have an obligation to take care of those who are ill or infirm, and that can happen to any of us. But we have an obligation to work as long as we're able, and that's a biblical principle too. He would say to me, "That's in your New Testament, Marc!"

In fact, the apostle Paul did say, "If anyone will not work, neither shall he eat" (2 Thess. 3:10). The work ethic is a part of Christianity. I've heard some people say that Jesus was a Socialist. The second chapter of Acts says that when the Holy Spirit came upon the Christian church, they shared all things in common, breaking bread together from house to house, pooling their resources communally as there was need. That's true. There was such a spirit of love and unity at the time that the people were eager to share their goods, but it was never a decree from Jesus that believers should give up what they own and go live in a worker's paradise. I believe it was Karl Marx who said that.

Somebody had to work to keep the resources coming in. You recall that Paul boasted that he continued to earn his wages by working at his trade as a tentmaker, even as he was traveling from town to town preaching the gospel. So the suggestion that Jesus meant for the church to become some sort of Socialist commune is false. But I'm fascinated by what Alexis de Tocqueville has to say in *Democracy in America*, speaking about the principle of "enlightened self-interest," or what he refers to in the book as "self interest rightly understood."[2]

During his journeys in this country, the French aristocrat was continually surprised by the spirit of benevolence he saw here. Rich and poor alike seemed to feel that it was their duty to participate in works of charity, pitching in to help a neighbor or providing assistance to other members of the community in times of need. He said the Americans he met, without exception, "enjoy explaining almost every act of their lives on the principle of self-interest properly understood. It gives them pleasure to point out how an enlightened self-interest occasionally leads them to help one another and disposes them freely to give part of their time and wealth for the good of the state."[3]

It would have been natural for a European traveler at the time to explain this sort of behavior as merely self-serving, "I'll-scratch-your-back-if-you-scratch-mine" behavior. But de Tocqueville quickly dismisses that option. Instead, he says, it has more to do with the almost universal Christian impulse of the people of this country. Later in the same book, he goes on to speak of that connection:

> Christianity does, it is true, teach that we must prefer others to ourselves in order to gain heaven. But Christianity also teaches that we must do good to our fellows for the love of God. That is a sublime utterance; man's mind filled with understanding of God's thought; to see that order is God's plan, in freedom labors for this great design, ever sacrificing his private interests for this wondrous ordering of all that is, and expecting no other reward than the joy of contemplating it.[4]

Philosophers from Helvetius and Locke to Adam Smith and Ayn Rand have dealt with the principle of enlightened self-interest, describing it as the basis of charity, cooperation, and political and social equality. Over the last ten years there has been a flurry of books on the order of Ted Baker's *Doing Well by Doing Good*, which takes a similar tack but suggests that corporations that find ways to serve their employees, customers, and other constituents, and demonstrate an interest in socially responsible activities, will not only do better on a personal level but will also do better financially as well, as their customers and suppliers respond to these efforts.[5]

THE INVISIBLE HAND

Prior to the Industrial Revolution we were still a European society, agrarian in nature, largely unemployed, and working for a landlord. You were born in labor, and you either owned land or you didn't. But the Industrial Revolution, which blossomed at the beginning of the nineteenth century in this country, changed all that. It urbanized the world. Within fifty years we were more urban than rural, more employed than unemployed, and wealth could be created in many new ways other than the old landlord-tenant relationships.

The United States was a great experiment in democracy and free enterprise, and we were part of all that, but we were a country with vast natural resources and an open-door policy that allowed people to come here and make a home without the burdens of the old feudal system. Even though land in the early days had been granted by European monarchs, it could be bought and sold. There was no king in America, and that was the second great experiment that Alexis de Tocqueville noted during his travels.

America was the first democratic society ever created by free men as a free and independent nation. China had existed for millennia, but was still a feudal system ruled by an emperor. Except for the idiosyncrasies of Asian culture, the economic structure of that nation was basically no different than the European model. So when the United States came on the scene, it changed the social, political, and economic dynamics of the entire world.

The fundamental assumption of our capitalist economy was the view that private enterprise is the most efficient way to organize a nation. In the great manifesto of the free-enterprise system, *The Wealth of Nations*, published incidentally in 1776, the Scottish economist and social philosopher Adam Smith wrote that the person who is free to borrow, lend, and conduct his own business is "led by an *invisible hand* to promote an end which was no part of his intention."[6] In free enterprise, he said, there is a sort of divine spirit transforming day-to-day commerce into something that benefits the entire community. Free enterprise and commerce work together by virtue of the Christian ethic that encourages mutual cooperation.[7]

Russia had been a Christian nation for nine hundred years before the 1917 Bolshevik Revolution came along and brought an end to private ownership. It was a kingdom under the

Russian czars, but there were commerce and a form of private ownership. In Great Britain, it was entrepreneurs working with the bankers and investment houses of the era that made the British Empire the greatest trading power on the earth in the eighteenth and nineteenth centuries. The king sanctioned it, and royal appointments were granted by the Crown, but the United States took it to the next level.

There is one other concept that is very important, and it's something every American should know. The Pilgrims, who risked everything to come here, were special people, led by their desire for religious freedom and a government that would balance the need for authority with personal liberty. They didn't want to overthrow the king. They weren't anarchists. They just wanted government to respect their right of self-determination. The language of the Declaration of Independence, the Constitution, and the Bill of Rights makes this so clear: the founders were seeking personal freedom within a society that provided mutual support and protection for all points of view.

As the population continued to grow and the colonies developed different economic, religious, and cultural identities, the citizens wanted to make sure their own interests would be protected. The Federalist Papers provide remarkable insight into the debates taking place at that time, describing what these early leaders thought about each other. In one case, a delegate from South Carolina told his family before leaving to go to New York to meet with the Continental Congress that he was giving the family a copy of his last will and testament in case he never returned. He was afraid of what might happen on the journey; it was like going to a foreign country. He didn't trust the people of New York, and he didn't want to go there. So, he said that if anything happened to him while he was away, they were free to administer his will as specified therein.

CHECKS AND BALANCES

In the Federalist Papers, James Madison expressed his concern that greedy and ambitious men would try to take advantage of their fellow countrymen, so the system of government they enacted needed to provide safeguards for the people. Goodwill and charity cannot be enforced by law, so in Federalist 51, he writes, "Ambition must be made to counteract ambition."[8] He recognized that the citizens of this new nation had competing interests, but they could insure fair and equal treatment by setting the various interests against each other. The most famous part of that document is where Madison writes the following:

> But what is government itself, but the greatest of all reflections on human nature? If men were angels, no government would be necessary. If angels were to govern men, neither external nor internal controls on government would be necessary. In framing a government which is to be administered by men over men, the great difficulty lies in this: you must first enable the government to control the governed; and in the next place oblige it to control itself.[9]

The problem, he argued, is that the people were afraid of an unaccountable federal bureaucracy, and the people of the various regions of the country didn't trust each other any better. They had many differences of opinion, but Madison said they could either exist separately and compete with one another, or they could bind themselves together as a constitutional republic that would provide security for everyone. But here's the concept that really struck home, and I believe it was a spiritual miracle. He said there would be more security for everyone if they were bound together, because then they could watch each other. That was such a remarkable concept. By watching each other and trusting the rule of law, they were finally able to agree on the provisions of the Constitution.

An Irish statesman during the founding era once made the observation that, "The condition upon which God hath given liberty to man is eternal vigilance; which condition if he break, servitude is at once the consequence of his crime."[10] Thomas Jefferson offered a slightly different version of that statement with the implication that free men must be as observant of their own government as they are of foreign powers and lawless tyrants.

In that regard, I remember an incident that happened when I was managing Pat Robertson's campaign in 1988. We had been debating abortion laws, and Pat argued that *Roe v. Wade* was a mistake. Justice Blackmun's majority opinion was based (as Justice William O. Douglas had argued in *Griswold v. Connecticut*) on emanations from the "penumbra of the First Amendment" that established a constitutional "right to privacy." A penumbra is a shadow, like the dark ring around the moon during an eclipse. There is no penumbra in the Constitution or the First Amendment; it's one of the most specific and unequivocal documents ever written, which is one of the hallmarks of its greatness. But this was where the liberal justices of the Supreme Court found the right to privacy that allows a mother to abort her unborn child.

When Pat pointed out the absurdity of that argument, the Left accused him of advocating lawlessness because he didn't accept the Court's reasoning. What Pat understood, however, was that the Supreme Court's ruling was bound only to the facts of the case. I remember one radio commentator saying, "Well, Pat Robertson thinks he can just run a stop sign if he wants to, because he doesn't want to obey the laws." But what that man failed to understand was that the Supreme Court is not the supreme law of the land; the Constitution is the supreme law of the land. I felt like calling the guy and saying, "Did you fail sixth-grade civics, or did you just miss class that day?" It's called "checks and balances." If the Court's rulings could be expanded beyond the facts of the case before them and actually become law, we would still have slavery today. The infamous Dred Scott ruling of 1857 is a lasting embarrassment to the Court and a reminder of what happens when Supreme Court justices try to legislate beyond the law.

There are three branches of government—legislative, judicial, and executive—and they're all controlled by the Constitution. The founders of our nation even worried about the risks of the elections process if certain people had undue influence, so they devised the Electoral College to ensure that a large majority of a region of the country didn't dominate in the selection of a president. It was sheer genius, and I would argue that such depth of reasoning and insight could only have come from God, as these men were seeking wisdom through prayer throughout the process of forming a government.

They had already won the revolution, and now they were trying to form a new nation, and the achievement was mind-boggling. This concept of checks and balances began with the Pilgrims, and it was instilled in our culture and mind-set. There's not that much about God in the Federalist Papers, but the entire spirit of those documents derives from the values and beliefs of the Pilgrims.

LOSING GROUND

The cement that holds the conservative coalition together is our mutual concern for freedom, balance, and limited government. Whether it's Christians seeking religious freedom or businessmen concerned about lower taxes and freedom from government interference, or foreign policy conservatives wanting the United States to remain strong in a time of global transition, we recognize that the burden rests with the people. We're the ones insisting on the freedom of the individual and limits on the authority of government. In Europe, government manages the resources of the people. But that's not the way we do it.

If we ever get to the point where 51 percent of the American people get their paycheck from the government, we will have entered a very different world. We're not there yet; the last time I looked it was roughly 33 percent. But many European countries are there now. If you include the bureaucracy, the military, law enforcement, public utilities, pension holders, and those on government support, you would quickly surpass the 50 percent mark in many countries. When we get to the point, as in France today, where more than 51 percent of the population derives their livelihood from the government, then a majority of the people will naturally vote for more and bigger government. Working for the common good will be a nonstarter.

The United States is still the only government that operates on the premise that government exists to encourage independence and free enterprise. Even Great Britain, which is one of the oldest democracies in the world—dating back to the Magna Carta in 1215, which recognized the autonomy of the people and placed restrictions on the authority of the king—is in danger of losing its way. Since the end of the Second World War and the expansion of the labor government, Britain has reversed course, and the economic engine of that nation is slowly grinding to a halt. As a result, many in Britain have their hand out to government.

In medieval times, Britain was the perfect model of a feudal system where everyone was in some sort of landlord-tenant relationship. They were born into a certain class, and that would never change. Whatever the people earned or produced belonged to the landlord, and whatever the landlord produced belonged to the Crown. Everyone was dependent upon the state for their welfare, and individual initiative was forcefully discouraged.

Most people were content with that relationship, but some, such as the Pilgrims, found it oppressive and emigrated to the New World where they would have freedom of thought and the opportunity to feed their families and conduct their affairs as they saw fit. America became a nation of people seeking freedom, and for the first three hundred years, that spirit remained very strong. We believed in individual liberty and autonomy and resisted the intrusion of government. But as we've matured as a nation, and as we've taken in larger and larger numbers of immigrants from third-world countries, we've lost some of that attitude.

We have a lot of people living here now who are apparently content to take their livelihood from the state. There are others who just want to put in their eight hours and get their paycheck each week. After thirty or forty years, they expect to get their pensions and just live out the rest of their lives. There's nothing wrong with that, I suppose. Not everyone can be an entrepreneur. But if you look at England or France, where half or more of the people take their livelihood from the state, you find that guaranteed minimum security isn't the greatest way to live. And the government still demands an enormous amount in taxes to meet its obligations.

PRESERVING THE CULTURE

When the settlers first came to Oklahoma over one hundred years ago in search of land, they weren't promised anything. They had the hope of getting free land, but they could also get shot doing it. They had no expectation that they could find a place to live. They would simply build some sort of basic structure as a home, then get up the next morning and work the fields. They couldn't petition the government for everything they needed and wouldn't have done so if they could. If they needed a horse or plow or seed for their crops, they had to figure out how to do it on their own. Nobody was going to do it for them. That attitude is a part of our heritage, and it's why Oklahomans are still so hardy and independent today.

People who've grown up in this way don't want government interfering in their business. But some of the people coming here from other parts of the world have seen our prosperity and want to be part of it. But many of them are under the impression they can get what they want from the government. They don't want to work for it; they want someone else to pay for it, and that creates all sorts of problems.

Every culture is designed to operate a certain way, and if it's successful, safe, and productive, the citizens and their government will work together to preserve the standards and values of the culture. At the very least, immigrants to this country need to learn our language, they need to become familiar with our history, and they need to learn how to live and conduct their affairs in ways that are appropriate for citizens of this nation.

They have every right to respect their native cultures and practice certain distinctive customs in their homes. But they have no right to expect the American people to change our customs, beliefs, or ways of doing things for their sake. Until they adjust to the American way of life, they are guests, and guests must respect the values and traditions of the host. If they can't abide by that most fundamental sign of respect, then they need to go back and start over. And that's just the way it is.

America, as the greatest social experiment in the history of the world, is a successful model that must be maintained as an island of freedom and opportunity in a sea of hidden agendas. Preserving our inheritance of personal liberty and free enterprise is essential if we expect to remain a beacon of freedom to the world. But we can't trust others to do this job for us. It will demand a personal commitment in the spirit of enlightened self-interest and the willingness to work for the common good.

Chapter 6

A BASE DIVIDED

Society is not something that is kept together physically; it is held by invisible bonds of common thought. If the bonds are too far relaxed the members would drift apart.[1]

—LORD PATRICK DEVLIN

The conservative movement that began to coalesce around Ronald Reagan's vision for America was a combination of an old and a new order. Prior to 1974, the base of the Republican Party was made up primarily of secular economic conservatives and foreign policy hawks. The economic perspective from the conservative side was that what's good for business is good for the country. For liberals, the argument was that organized labor must keep big business honest. Benefits for workers were still defined in terms of pensions and wages, and the debate in Congress was all about Europeanization and the big-government model.

Big business, big government, and big labor working in concert to manage the country's resources for the benefit of all—that all sounded a bit too much like something out of George Orwell's *1984* for most conservatives, but that was the way the argument went. The parameters and framework of the discussion assumed that the European model was the only logical basis for our economic future. Whatever flaws we may have detected in the policies of Britain, France, or Germany simply had to be amended for our particular needs.

Prior to 1974, there was little discussion of small-business needs in the U.S. economy. Small business operated under the radar, not as an underground industry, just unnoticed. Confirmation of this fact can be seen in the way the United States Department of Commerce defined small business as late as 1993. After the 1988 election cycle, Robert Mosbacher became the United States Secretary of Commerce. Bob and I had become good friends during President Bush's campaign, and I was looking forward to working with him again.

Secretary Mosbacher was my liaison, along with Lee Atwater, for introducing new Christian activists to the Bush campaign. We were in contact throughout the Bush 41 administration. I discovered the value of small-business owners as a political network in much the same way I had discovered the Christian Right, by being involved directly with campaigns at the state level. In the 1990 cycle, I was executive director of the National Republican Congressional Committee (NRCC). Presidential consultant Ed Rollins was cochair along with Representative Guy Vander Jagt. Ed proved to be a brilliant leader as we sought new themes for this off-year election.

Bubbling up in Republican campaigns all over the country at that time were groups of dissatisfied small-business owners who felt like they were overtaxed and overregulated. As we talked to business owners around the country, this became a recurring theme, and we realized that it could also be a good foundation for expanding the size of the conservative coalition.

In late 1989 and early 1990, we conducted extensive survey research to analyze the decision-making process of the electorate from a variety of different viewpoints. We found that large segments of voters were changing their opinions of how they defined themselves and what issues were most important to them. The changes in attitude and identification could be tracked all the way back to 1974. For the first time, we realized just how large the community of small-business owners was, how many people they employed, and most importantly, we found that the average number of employees who worked in small businesses was fewer than twenty-five.

The U.S. Department of Commerce at the time defined a small business as fifteen hundred employees or less. And further, their analysts believed that the number of small businesses in the United States that had twenty-five or fewer employees would be around 5 percent. The irony is that this miscalculation was almost identical to the error journalists had in their analysis of evangelical Christians as a percentage of the population.

THE ECONOMIC CONSTITUENCY

The fact is, fully 80 percent of all businesses in the United States have twenty-five employees or less, employing 45 percent of the nonfarm adult workforce. I actually took our research to the skeptical research division at the Department of Commerce to confirm that our numbers were correct. Following the growth of the National Federation of Independent Business (NFIB), under the leadership of Jack Faris, the size and impact of small business is now a well-known fact.

Prior to 1974, there was little or no discussion of religious issues in politics. It was just not something people talked about. Most Christians didn't think of themselves in political terms. We just thought of ourselves as either conservatives, blue-collar workers, or people who just happened to have an interest in foreign policy. Barry Goldwater, who has been referred to as the father of modern conservatism, didn't pay much attention to social issues. In fact, later in life he actually espoused Libertarian views on social issues. But after the appearance of Ronald Reagan on the national political scene, blue-collar Catholics began to unite with foreign policy conservatives and occasionally with social conservatives. That was the beginning of the movement.

In the beginning, this new Reagan coalition had a common bond in the definition of *conservatism*. It was the embryonic stages of moving the debate away from the focus on European structures toward solutions that focused on the ideas and interests of our own country. In Europe, religion continued to decline. Church attendance had fallen to nearly nothing, and the idea that faith could provide a meaningful worldview was rapidly disappearing. Appeasement toward the Soviet Union was as strong as ever, and the defense of Socialism and the managed-economy model was their main consideration.

After 1974, a restructuring and expansion of the grass roots added to this Old World movement. The Christian Right and the New Right expanded to the individual their ability to become active conservatives. The supply-side Right was more of an academic movement that challenged the conventional thinking that emanated from the ivory tower and the college elite. This idea that government could take less of our earnings and actually generate more for the government coffers was a revolutionary thought for conservatives and pure heresy for liberals.

The conservative idea was that if you give people more freedom, there will be more for everyone to work with, including government. But that's not really what the liberals wanted. They feared letting go of their control over the people and the processes of government. Liberals do not trust individuals to make decisions for themselves in their own best interest that will, in the end, benefit the greater good of all. Then as now, they're determined to control our lives by government policies and regulations rather than simply allowing government to facilitate the potential of each individual.

The idea that you could actually limit government by giving it less taxing ability and enhancing individual liberty, then ending up with more funding for government services, was the rallying cry that catapulted Ronald Reagan into the White House. Much like the old-style conservative coalition prior to 1974 and post–World War II, there was a new compatibility among the groups who agreed that limited government and individual liberty should be the goals of the movement.

Small-business owners weren't actually organized politically as small-business owners until the late 1980s, but they were beginning to self-identify based on their vocational and professional interests, which would eventually lead to the development of their own professional associations and a grassroots movement. This coming together of like-minded conservatives was driven by two characteristics of small-business owners. Most of these people had always been economic conservatives, but what they discovered was that they were also social conservatives and the majority were born-again Christians.

They understood that their survival depended on less government intervention in their businesses. These were the very ones who would be hurt the most if the academics, experts, and other liberal groups insisted on pushing the United States government toward a European system. The fact that they were conservatives, not only economically but also socially, was not known until the NFIB conducted an extensive research project on small-business ownership in order to prepare for the 1994 election cycle.

A UNIFIED PURPOSE

This research was critical to understanding the reaction of small business to Hillary Clinton's proposed health-care plan. It was a reaction to this health-care plan and the ability of NFIB's leadership to respond to small business's demand for change that, in part, led to the Republican takeover of Congress that year for the first time in forty years. It's important to note that NFIB was then, and is now, truly nonpartisan and unbiased in its approach to national politics. It simply responds to its members' demands.

Their agenda is driven by their membership. It was this absolute rule that they are a member-driven organization that left them as the only group standing that opposed Hillary's health-care plan. In 1994, small businesses felt threatened economically and culturally, just as Christians did in 1974. A threat to your culture means that you're feeling the risk of a negative change to your way of life. In this case, they were afraid of being forced out of business.

All of the divisions of the old- and new-order conservative movements still exist today. However, they are reexamining themselves in reference to the future and the global forces looming out there on the horizon. These challenges are much more imposing and have a very different character than the national forces we've faced over the last forty years. The leadership of the older groups are retiring now and passing from the scene. The boomer generation is at or near retirement age, and a generation of new and younger leaders is developing in the Christian Right, the New Right, and the foreign-policy Right.

These people view things somewhat differently, and they're not in lockstep with their predecessors. For instance, some of today's evangelical leaders are advocating social justice programs encompassing poverty, the global war on AIDS, and climate change. Many now feel that the environment should be one of the main priorities of Christians who want to make an impact on the culture. There is a lot of debate about these proposals, however, and serious questions are being raised about the orthodoxy of some of the movement leaders, such as Jim Wallis, Richard Cizik, Rick Warren, and others.[2]

This leadership has not yet given an opinion on how Christians should be involved in government to achieve all these admirable goals. In a newly released book titled *The Great Awakening*, liberal theologian Jim Wallis writes about reviving faith in politics in the post–religious Right era. He calls those Christians who want to take action to fight poverty, clean up the environment, and find cures for AIDS and other diseases "the silent majority of religious Americans."[3] He believes this new generation of the faithful will have to begin by taking action in their own local communities. But at the moment their influence is still relatively small.

I don't know whether or not these young people are a majority, but they claim to be a substantial segment of the religious community. But just as the old-world conservatives didn't go away, neither will those who believe in the traditional principles and goals of the Christian Right. What's taking place is not a change in the grass roots so much as it is a restructuring. And just as Christians were a major part of society prior to 1974 but only marginally involved in the political arena, they suddenly discovered themselves in politics after 1974. They've made a big difference ever since, and who's to say their successors may not do the same?

Small-business owners had always been a part of the American economy, but it wasn't until 1993 when they began to feel their livelihoods were threatened that they came into their own politically. There's certainly nothing wrong with the political agenda of the Christian Right, but it may become a smaller component and a somewhat small component of Christian activity in this country in the future. If what the Reagan coalition believed in 1980 was the truth, then it's still the truth today. If it wasn't eternal then, it wasn't the truth but merely an opinion. Opinions can change, but the truth never changes. It's important not just that one defines the truth for oneself, but that he makes a personal commitment to determine what truth is.

In the presidential cycle of 2008, the base is further divided than ever. This is very remarkable and the first time I've seen it this way. There is no obvious charismatic leader for the Reagan coalition. From 1980 through 2004, right up to the end of the last forty-year cycle, we were comfortable in the knowledge that there was always a Reagan coalition leader when we needed one. We didn't have to work very hard to feel secure in our positions or in our places in Reagan's big tent. We were used to hearing the same themes, the same messages, and the same answers to our questions. Now we find a field of candidates who are partly right and partly wrong, and nobody is entirely happy with the ones we have to choose from.

The issues facing our country today are of a global nature. Some readers will no doubt remember the turbulent times of the late-1960s when national issues were so unsettling. We were living in the euphoria of a dynamic economy with the peace dividend that followed the end of World War II. But global issues were challenging us, we were in the middle of the cold war, and the university campuses were literally on fire with protests of every kind, from the free-love movement to the incessant howls of antiwar radicals protesting the Vietnam War. That era, thankfully, is gone. But today, after the collapse of the Soviet Union and with the advancement of free trade and creation of the World Trade Organization, we find ourselves in another welter of controversy and in desperate need of a strong conservative leader.

RETHINKING RELATIONSHIPS

To my knowledge, only one evangelical leader endorsed the candidacy of former New York Mayor Rudy Giuliani in the 2008 campaign—Pat Robertson. For many Christians, this endorsement is very perplexing. Mayor Giuliani does not share the values of a sizable portion of the Reagan coalition, let alone Robertson's Christian Right. He is pro-choice, pro-gay rights, and pro-gun control. One evangelical leader told me he could never support the Giuliani campaign because of the positions Giuliani has taken on those issues.

Later, when Senator Sam Brownback, an evangelical, dropped his presidential bid in 2007, he endorsed Senator John McCain, who has expressed hostility toward the faith community. Mayor Giuliani has endorsed Senator McCain. Whether or not John McCain is successful in this campaign, the emotion causes great consternation among many on the religious Right when there are divisions of this sort in our own ranks.

Other conservatives, including many who are primarily focused on social and moral issues, came out strongly in support of former candidate Mitt Romney. But while these members of the coalition may support his positions on a wide range of issues, they will have to make some accommodation for his Mormon faith. In chapter 3 I discussed briefly how this could be accomplished, but it will require a conscious act of will to continue in that vein in the future.

Governor Mike Huckabee has struck a resonant chord with many conservative Christians and has made a strong showing in state primaries and caucuses. He has demonstrated a remarkable ability to communicate in a personable and charismatic manner; people feel comfortable with him and trust him. As the depth and extent of the current recession is calculated, Huckabee will be measured more by his economic programs and policies, but his rise to the top tier of Republican contenders has opened a lot of people's eyes.

New Right conservatives have many choices and are less concerned about the religious beliefs of the candidates. But they too have expressed concern when the leaders of their coalition seem to be endorsing candidates who aren't strictly of their own persuasion on the issues. The base that was accustomed to following their leaders' advice must now learn how to think for themselves. More than likely they will give their support to leaders with whom they have a connection or some ongoing familiarity, as they did in 1974. But, again, adjustments will have to be made.

Foreign policy conservatives are having difficulty today explaining to their peers why America should stay the course in Iraq, much as their predecessors did in the early 1970s following the collapse of the Vietnam War. The war in Iraq, as controversial as it has been, did not involve a draft. Had there been a draft requiring people to go to war against their will, I suspect we would have seen many more protests and a lot more hostility. The choice of a candidate for members of this wing of the conservative movement will depend largely on whom they believe can best confront, contain, and defeat terrorism. It is this group who has helped propel Senator McCain to the nomination of the Republican Party for president of the United States. And that debate resonates with other parts of the movement as well.

The most frustrated component of the new-order conservatives is the economic conservatives. They're the ones who fought hard for a Republican majority in Congress and feel they have very little to show for it. It's not the war and its expense so much as it's the expanded government programs and the huge increases in spending. As was the case with Richard Nixon's implementation of price controls, economic conservatives today feel abandoned, and they're angered by the administration's and

Congress' apparent insensitivity to the need to control spending. They felt that if deficits were increased because of the war in Iraq, their leaders should have given the impression that they were concerned. But that commitment never came.

Economic conservatives and advocates for the free-enterprise system have embraced the concept of free trade. Milton Friedman was an outspoken advocate of free trade who believed that if any country uses protectionism to develop its markets, they will ultimately pay the price as their protected but inefficient markets become noncompetitive and implode in upon themselves. In a new book called *Day of Reckoning*, former presidential candidate Pat Buchanan takes a very different point of view and writes that uncontrolled free trade will destroy key manufacturing sectors and ultimately jeopardize our national security.[4]

Free trade should be managed strategically, Buchanan says, in accordance with the national interest. Pat Buchanan is a respected conservative leader, and his voice can be very persuasive since he commands a large and active following. Differences of opinion within the Reagan coalition over economic matters are as critical to the base of the party as the split among evangelicals over the choice of a presidential contender. But they haven't divided the coalition or made the voice of the Right any less effective.

The question generating the most heat among free-trade conservatives is whether or not a Communist country such as China can be seen as a good corporate citizen in the global free-enterprise community. China is a Communist country that has become a member of the World Trade Organization and still runs its government-owned corporations from a nonmarket viewpoint with a Socialist political agenda, coupled with a culture that allows totalitarian control. But can such a system ever be compatible with a free-trade economy?

REMARKABLE PROSPERITY

After the 1976 presidential cycle, Ronald Reagan again announced for the Republican presidential bid but was by no means the obvious choice. As I indicated earlier, the new conservative coalition hadn't been established as a political movement at that time. The national press didn't accept it, and the liberal elite tried to deny it for fear that it might be real.

As I mentioned in chapter 1, several candidates ran in that Republican primary on the simple premise that Ronald Reagan could never be nominated or elected; therefore, they said, I must step in and run so the people will be able to have the choices they desire. With the divisions in Republican ranks in the 2008 election, we may see that same decision by a third-party candidate in this race as well. At least two of the candidates in the race for president have unprecedented negatives. And they're hard negatives. By that I mean that individuals in the polls are saying, "I will not vote for this candidate under any circumstances." But despite the negative numbers, these third-party candidates still have a chance of being nominated and elected.

At the writing of this book, the candidate most rumored to be considering a third-party run is the mayor of New York, Michael Bloomberg. He will run as a nonpartisan advocate of common-ground solutions and will have the support of elected Democratic and Republican officials. If, in fact, he does run, the Electoral College will become very complicated, possibly throwing the election into the House of Representatives. In deciding whom to support for president, one should apply the grid to the candidate and his policies and make your decision based upon freedom and accountability.

A divided coalition can result in a person being elected president who believes in managed government and the Europeanization of America. This will take us down the path toward government control and a system that attempts to provide everything you need or desire as you give up all of your freedom. As the people become more dependent upon government services, they will be required to yield more and more servitude to the state. This is basically what F. A. Hayek warned about in his book *The Road to Serfdom*. Hayek believed that "the collectivist idea of empowering government with increasing economic control would inevitably lead not to a Utopia but to the horrors of Nazi Germany and Fascist Italy."[5]

Each division must understand that the core essential value to the energy of the movement is freedom, less government, trusting the individual and innovation over government control and regulation, and each man and woman doing for themselves and their family what they feel best for their prosperity. The end goal of each division is in no way in conflict. Social conservatives have no problem with a strong national defense. Foreign policy hawks have no problem with free enterprise. Christian Right activists have no problem with lower taxes. And in the next new conservative order, solving the problems of AIDS, the environment, and poverty have no conflict with any of the above. What is tantamount to each division is that a government-managed, controlled, European system will destroy or hinder certain key aspects of American culture that are unique in the world.

Just as Ronald Reagan led us into the possibility of a free environment unthreatened by government, we must maintain the United States as the only country in the world that still stands proudly as an island of prosperity in a sea of Socialist decay. If Europeanization is the end result of our great experiment in democracy and individual liberty, every one of these divisions of American conservatism will have failed, and none of us will attain our goals.

Whenever I pause to think that this country in just over two hundred years has built this enormous infrastructure of roads and utilities, I'm absolutely amazed. There is probably no place in the United States that doesn't have indoor plumbing if they want it. That's just incredible. Having running water and indoor plumbing in terrain of every sort—mountains, deserts, and plains—is as incredible to me as the pyramids and everything else. How many places in the world have I been to where those things are literally unimaginable?

The Chinese people like to boast that they have six thousand years of history, while America has just over two hundred years. But look what we've achieved in that time. In 2007 my home state of Oklahoma celebrated one hundred years of statehood. And in that relatively short span of time we have power and utilities in every single city and town in the state. We have streets and infrastructure and rural electricity, and the mail gets delivered. There is no place in the state where those basic things aren't available. How did that happen?

Nothing like that ever happened in Russia or China or Africa, even though they have thousands of years more history than we do. I would submit that it was because they haven't been able to develop governments that trust the people to be innovative and take care of themselves, either individually or collectively, for the greater good. In this country, all of us are allowed to follow our instincts and pursue happiness as we see fit, acting independently. That, I believe, is the way God intended it to be. We are to keep the Judeo-Christian laws, which were designed by Him for our good, not as a controlling God but as a loving God who knows what's good for us. If we keep those laws, I believe we will continue to prosper.

A REMARKABLE ASSESSMENT

When I think about the uniqueness of the American experiment in democracy, I often wonder when this remarkable combination will spread to other countries around the globe. Can you imagine what it would be like if most of the world shared our enthusiasm for freedom of thought, free enterprise, and religious liberty? What would it mean if countries like China and Russia, for example, ever bought into this vision of freedom and prosperity? And for that matter, what if those countries allowed their citizens to worship as Christians, without fear of reprisal? How would that change the world?

Former *TIME* magazine correspondent and best-selling author David Aikman made a trip to China in 2002, going back to many of the places where he had traveled as *TIME*'s bureau chief in Beijing. David is a devout Christian, and he was especially interested in seeing what was happening in the house churches and the other underground churches, to find whether or not religion was having any real impact in that country. What he saw was truly remarkable, so much so that he decided to write a book about it. The result is a work called *Jesus in Beijing: How Christianity Is Changing the Global Balance of Power*, and it's a fascinating read.

Shortly before the book came out, David gave a lecture at the Ethics and Public Policy Center in Washington, in which he talked about his journey and the things he discovered. He said that the underground churches are thriving, and by some estimates there may be as many as two hundred million believers in China today. That's a shocking number, and if that's actually the case, it would mean that roughly 20 percent of all Chinese adults are Bible-believing Christians.

The most surprising story David told at that event, however, involved a conversation that he and another friend had with the outgoing head of state, Jiang Zemin, who had been president of China and general secretary of the Communist Party. At one point in the interview, Jiang was asked what he would wish for his country now that he was no longer its leader. Would it be economic prosperity, military superiority, a greater share of the global economy? Much to the visitor's surprise, the Communist leader said, "I would like for my country to become a Christian nation."[6]

That was the one answer no one had expected. Ever since Mao Zedong founded the Chinese Communist Party in 1921, religion in any form has been strictly forbidden there. So the interviewer quickly asked, "Why?" As it turned out, a panel of Chinese scholars had spent twenty years trying to find out why China continually lagged so far behind the West in science, industry, and culture. After considering every possible explanation, they realized that it was the religious heritage of the West that had allowed us to rise to such heights.

David Aikman includes a fascinating transcription of how that came about in his book, where one of China's leading scholars offers this remarkable assessment:

> One of the things we were asked to do was to look into was what accounted for the success, in fact, the pre-eminence of the West all over the world. We studied everything we could from the historical, political, economic, and cultural perspective. At first, we thought it was because you had more powerful guns than we had. Then we thought it was because you had the best political system. Next we focused on your economic systems. But in the past twenty years, we have realized that the heart of your culture is your religion: Christianity. This is why the West is so powerful. The Christian moral foundation of social and cultural life was what made possible the emergence of capitalism and then the successful transition to democratic politics. We don't have any doubt about this.[7]

This was clearly the assessment that Jiang Zemin had made. There is only one thing that could make such a difference: America is a Christian nation. China is not. What the elder statesman realized, no doubt, was that if Christianity could do so much for us, then he wanted the same thing for his own country. That wise old man had put his finger on it. The most remarkable thing about our own experiment in democracy, as I've said repeatedly, is that the principles of religious liberty and free enterprise first came together on these shores, and that incredible combination has literally changed the world.

THE RUSSIAN SOLUTION

Wouldn't it be wonderful if all the leaders of the great nations of the world were as open-minded and forward thinking as that Chinese leader? No one can be certain how that conversation turned out, or what might become of President Zemin's wish for his country. But something is happening in China today, as my friend David Aikman reports. For now we understand that there's still persecution of Christians in that country, and free enterprise isn't doing all that well, despite the fact that China's government-controlled export companies are doing a land-office business with America's largest discount stores.

But what about that other nemesis, Russia, and the former land-office countries? Several years ago I was on a diplomatic mission to Russia, and a member of President Boris Yeltsin's team came to me with the question: "Who can we bring in to teach ethics?" In Russian society, as in any Communist state, the citizens are constantly defending themselves against the state. Most of the time, people have to live by their wits, so if they come across something lying on the ground that doesn't belong to them, it's considered public property. No one owns it, so people just pick it up and take it home. Tools disappear from the job site and food vanishes from shelves because there's no ethical basis for making people understand even the simplest principles of the Ten Commandments.

The Russian people needed some basic understanding of why they shouldn't steal the tools and loaves of bread, and this carries over into many other areas. If there were security guards or policemen on the premises, they could control the people's behavior through fear and intimidation, but that wasn't a very satisfactory situation. What they needed was a value system that changes people's motivations and teaches them to respond instinctively in an ethical and honest manner, which is, of course, one of the consummate values of the Christian faith.

When they asked how we accomplished this sort of thing in America, I told them it was our Judeo-Christian values, enshrined in our basic constitutional system of government by the Founding Fathers. When they had considered my words, the Russian president's staff arranged to have Christian teachers from the United States brought over to lecture in Russian schools and universities to teach the people essential moral principles. Oklahoma Baptist University did this for a time, holding workshops in Moscow and various other places.

A pertinent question to ask at this point is, what did Jesus ever ask proactively of the government? The answer is nothing. His kingdom was and is not of this system of things. He faced government. He didn't back down from government. But He asked nothing of government. Did Jesus ever ask us to take over the government and Christianize the nation? No. Is the point of Christianity to Christianize the nation? No. The point of Christianity is to evangelize and present the Word of God as we understand it, as handed down from Jesus and the apostles. Our goal is not to enforce our religious values on the nation but simply to practice our faith freely as the Constitution allows, knowing that the gospel is quick and powerful and sharper than any two-edged sword.

True faith can transform a nation and heal the divisions between us. But it must be freely chosen and freely applied. When government imposes on that freedom, we have a moral imperative to maintain the balance between freedom and government so that our children and each generation after us can inherit the same environment of freedom that we inherited. It's essential to be able to present our beliefs in such a way that people can make the decision for themselves.

French president Nicolas Sarkozy addressed a joint session of Congress on November 7, 2007. In that speech, he said, "America can count on France," and described America this way:

> America did not tell the millions of men and women who came from every country in the world and who—with their hands, their intelligence and their heart—built the greatest nation in the world: "Come, and everything will be given you." She said: "Come, and the only limits to what you'll be able to achieve will be your own courage and your own talent." America embodies this extraordinary ability to grant each and every person a second chance.
>
> Here, both the humblest and most illustrious citizens alike know that nothing is owed to them and that everything has to be earned. That's what constitutes the moral value of America. America did not teach men the idea of freedom; she taught them how to practice it. And she fought for this freedom whenever she felt it to be threatened somewhere in the world. It was by watching America grow that men and women understood that freedom was possible.[8]

What made America great, as the French president wisely stated, was her ability to transform her own dreams into hope for all mankind. If countries like China, Russia, and France can see it, you have to wonder why our own citizens remain so divided. Unless we can come together in one accord to bring about a new consensus of like-minded men and women who cherish the promise of freedom, our prospects for the century ahead may look bleak indeed. We have the resources, and we have the opportunity in this election year to turn a corner. The only question is, will we remain an island of freedom, and will the rest of the world be able to count on us to lead the way?

Chapter 7

THE CHALLENGE OF GLOBALISM

Kites rise highest against the wind, not with it.[1]
—WINSTON CHURCHILL

I think it's incredible that nearly a half century after Reagan's speech at the Republican Convention, the debates between advocates of a managed economy and supporters of a free-enterprise economy are once again issues in presidential politics. This time, however, they're not just issues for the voters in our country; they're also hotly debated topics around the world. The global economy is in the midst of massive transition as a result of new technologies, advanced communications, and the emergence of new global trade organizations, and this is something that's going to be a major challenge in the years ahead.

The United States consumes roughly half of the world's goods today. Western Europe consumes another thirty percent. This means that, together, the eight countries identified as the G8 industrialized nations consume 80 percent of all goods produced on the earth. Yet, more and more of that production is coming from China, India, and other Asian countries. Never before in history have so many goods been manufactured in one area of the world for consumption by the individuals in another.

Multinational corporations now have the ability to manufacture the component parts of their products in many different locations, with final assembly taking place somewhere other than the point of manufacture. Advanced software systems developed over the last ten years allow for this sort of diversified manufacturing process. In the past, manufacture and assembly had to take place, or at least be coordinated, under one roof. But that's no longer the case. Now the component parts of a piece of machinery or an electronic device can be manufactured wherever the manufacturer feels he can get the best deal.

In most cases final assembly is then completed close to the consumer—in this case, the United States and Europe. Because of this, "just-in-time" manufacturing and assembly plants are becoming the wave of the future for products distributed in North America. These new systems are changing the way cargo is shipped to the United States as well as how it's distributed when it arrives. Already we're seeing an increased use of air cargo as a major transportation option in the production of overseas goods.

To alleviate congestion at the nation's port facilities, rail carriers are devising plans to take containers straight from port of entry to rail, and then transporting them to inland ports for distribution by truck to their final destination. For the first time ever, there is now a market for air-to-rail and rail-to-air cargo connecting suppliers halfway around the world to retail outlets in this country.

All this innovation is made possible by the enormous scale of the global economy and the vast wealth generated by international manufacturing and trade. The United States is still the largest and most reliable producer in the global economy; however, large accumulations of capital are developing in two other strategically important parts of the world: in China because of the huge increases in manufacturing in that country, and in the Middle East because of the high price of oil.

The transfer of capital between countries has an impact on interest rates in the United States, and sudden shifts in the marketplace—such as labor costs, for example, or abrupt changes in diplomatic relations between trading partners— can affect the stability of the U.S. dollar and create volatility in the global markets. This, in turn, impacts the flow of currency, the stability of the marketplace overall, as well as the value of stocks and bonds on Wall Street.

THE INTERNATIONALIST AGENDA

As the United States and Europe continue to lead the world in consumption, they have also become the leading "debtor nations" in the global economy. Regardless of the debate over free trade versus protected trade, the liberal view of meeting the current and inevitable transition of economic forces is to increase controls and attempt to manage the economy as it is today in Europe. As the pressures on international trade increase, there is a tendency for government to increase its meddling, which results in a gradual creep toward Europeanization.

So what does a European-style managed economy mean to you? The organizations that are pushing hardest for this model are the labor unions. Organized labor sees a world coordinated by United Nations committees, where collective bargaining can be managed on a standardized system worldwide. Wages paid to workers in countries—from Vietnam and China to Venezuela, Mexico, Russia, Europe, and the United States— would all be orchestrated by a handpicked group of monetary "experts" and regulators. This model seems to appeal to the leaders of big labor.

Already, overtures have been made to China, the United States, and the United Nations for globalized collective bargaining. American trade unions have gone so far in this Congress as to interfere with trade treaties they disagree with that have already been negotiated by the United States trade ambassador's office and agreed to by the leadership of the Democratic Congress. This is unheard of, but the trend will continue if the United States pursues a course of managed government.

How does this expansion of global markets impact the cultural way of life in the United States? Fifty percent of the nonfarm adult workforce either owns or works for a company of twenty-five employees or less. Small businesses generated 80 percent of the new jobs created in the United States in the past ten years. As the United States has gone through this transformation of the world's economic infrastructure, the small-business sector has kept the U.S. productivity and its job expansion rising. But the pressures on small-business owners are increasing daily.

This economic complex of large and small businesses working together to produce innovation, efficiency, quality, cost control, and safety in the American economy is unique to the world. It works and enhances not only small business but also large manufacturers. Every company, from Boeing to AT&T to IBM to General Electric to General Motors, uses small-business suppliers, vendors, contractors, and installers to make their business systems and production methods more competitive. This gives American-based multinational companies a competitive edge over their rivals in capturing multibillion dollar contracts.

The reason small business thrives in the United States is because it is free to innovate. A small-business entrepreneur in the United States can do what he or she wants as long as it is legal. That's another benefit of the free-enterprise system. Business owners don't have to first get permission from some faraway government entity. Compare that to trade practices in most other countries. Just getting permission in most countries, even if it's forthcoming, can take weeks and sometimes months, and costs thousands of dollars.

So who are these small-business owners? They're the people on Main Street in big cities and small towns all across America. They're the people who support the local band, the orchestra, and the high school football teams. They're the men and women who man the sign-in tables at the church auction and the voting booths at your local polling place. They're the people who care about the local community.

They are also the last segment of society that the American public trusts. When asked in survey research, "Whom do you trust to tell you the truth on complicated issues?" the one entity the American public most consistently identify as the ones they're most likely to believe are small-business owners. This is because people don't believe that small-business owners would do anything to hurt the communities in which they're doing business.

Most small-business owners live in the communities they serve, so they naturally have a commitment to the citizens of the area. They participate in local events, send their kids to local schools, and have many interests in common with their neighbors. The major political parties, national polling and consulting firms, and research organizations of all kinds are continually searching for any category of people they can define that can add credibility to their political interests and motivations. Obviously, the politicians they serve are eager to gain the trust of the American public. What they consistently find is that the two groups most people in this country trust most often are the small-business owners and farmers.

TENETS OF EUROPEANIZATION

What are the tenets of managed government and Europeanization? They include a long list of government mandates that determine how employers relate to their employees and how they conduct their business affairs. They include such things as government-mandated pensions, health-care protection, set workweek hours, and restrictions on layoffs and firings. It takes a certain economy of scale to be able to provide all the benefits these mandates require. But in a European-style managed economy, few exemptions are given for small business.

Whether the number of employees is one hundred or fifteen hundred may depend upon the industry they serve, but high-cost government-mandated benefits programs are often larger than small-business owners can afford. The argument that small-business owners should be forced to provide certain benefits (or else simply go out of business) destroys the whole basis of new business formation, which is so essential to innovation and growth.

Further, such mandates infringe on the small-business owner's ability to run his or her business. In some European countries business owners must give sixty days notice before they can lay off an employee, whether they have just cause or not. Then they must be able to pay certain benefits for that worker for an extended period of time. For the government to get this involved in how people run their businesses is non-sensical if not economically criminal. In a world in the midst of massive transition and global competition, the business owners need to be able to determine the policies that best suit the workplace environment. Flexibility is essential.

Liberals who believe in managed economies don't even trust the programs they establish. If small-business owners didn't pay their employees well enough and larger corporations were creating jobs that paid better, the workers would go out immediately and take those jobs. This is the kind of competition that makes the marketplace model successful. It takes both large and small businesses working in concert to compete successfully in a global economy, creating jobs for individuals and wealth for the nation.

Another way to put the debate is to ask the question, which do you trust: innovation or regulation? Do you really believe that a government bureaucrat who has never signed the front of a paycheck can best determine by regulation how to manage change better than the entrepreneur acting freely in a free society? The small-business owner is risking his or her own capital, knowing full well that if he or she isn't successful with his or her ideas and products and service to the community, his or her family won't eat.

In 1993, the country got a preview of the consequences of a managed economy and Europeanization. Hillary Rodham Clinton chaired for the president of the United States, her husband, Bill Clinton, a task force to develop universal health care in the United States. After months of debate and hearings, Mrs. Clinton and her chief administrator, Ira Magaziner, proposed a health-care plan that literally would have put a majority of small-business owners out of business. Health-care plans and their costs would have been mandated by law in the United States no matter what size with very few exemptions.

The cost of health care for large businesses would be moved to the American taxpayer in a national health-care system. Let's think about that for a minute: You are an executive officer of General Motors; your bonus is based upon increased profits year on year pursuant to a calendar year; your company has accumulated legacy costs of $2 billion for health-care guarantees for current and retired employees. If this legislation had passed with one stroke of a pen, those costs would have been removed from GM's contingency liabilities to the American taxpayer with a small percent going to the small-business owner with no consideration being given as to whether they could pay for them.

In the next calendar year, GM's bottom line profits are increased by the amount of money not obligated to health-care costs. It amounts to hundreds of millions of dollars. Large business did not ask for it, but they would certainly take it. When asked about this result and consequence and the exposure to small business at a business roundtable luncheon, it is reported that a spokesman for the plan said, "I cannot be held accountable for every undercapitalized small business in the United States." This showed absolute disregard and insensitivity to a unique cultural component of our society which includes fully 50 percent of the population.

THE RISKS OF HILLARY CARE

The National Federation of Independent Business (NFIB) is the United States' largest small-business organization. The president of the organization during the 1994 debates over nationalized health care was S. Jackson Faris. I was acting as the vice president of political affairs for that organization at the time. We had been organizing small-business owners into an effective political force, going state by state to build a constituency. NFIB at one point was the only organization in Washington that opposed Hillary Clinton's health-care plan. Although we were under enormous pressure, Jack and his team did not yield. We knew that passage of the plan would have destroyed small business in this country.

I tried to explain the ramifications and consequences of the plan to national news media, describing the effect it would have on small business. I had great difficulty in convincing the reporters and broadcasters that it was an issue of great concern in every state. I eventually invited a well-known national reporter to a hearing that we were sponsoring in Phoenix, Arizona. I asked her what she thought would be a good turnout for such a hearing that, if the media were correct, no one cared about.

I reminded her that it was difficult to get fifty people to a meeting with a United States senator for a town hall meeting, and I think she thought that we would only get forty or fifty middle-aged people with a lot of time on their hands. But I was honest with her, and I told her we expected two hundred fifty people to show up, and all the arrangements at the venue were set up for that number. When we got to the hearing, there were more than five hundred people waiting for us when we arrived, and more were standing outside demanding to be let in. Not only was the crowd attentive, they were angry about what they were hearing from Washington. Needless to say, this remarkable turnout got the reporter's attention.

The business owners of Phoenix didn't need us to explain what was wrong with Hillary Care; they just wanted to know what we were going to do about it. They already knew that if that health-care plan passed as drafted, they were out of business, and their way of life would have been destroyed. That meeting helped to launch a series of front-page articles about how destructive this plan would have been to grassroots America. Before long, other organizations climbed onto the bandwagon with NFIB, and Hillary's disastrous plan was ultimately defeated.

There are really two stories here: One is that the designers of the universal health-care plan did not understand the impact of that type of nationalized mandate on the key cultural institutions of this country. They hadn't even considered that the dramatically escalating costs being forced down the throats of business owners would have dealt a deathblow to tens of thousands of small businesses. And the destruction of small business would have made all business in the United States less competitive. Without the presence of small business, millions of jobs would have simply disappeared—right in the middle of one of the greatest transitions in the history of world economics.

Make no mistake; this bad health-care plan would have impacted all of us in many ways. Unelected bureaucrats would have been appointed at the county level as county health-care commissioners. They would have been given the authority to determine the priority of health-care services, deciding which individuals would receive health care and which would be denied. In other words, someone in their nineties might not get surgery for certain serious ailments, while someone younger who needed treatment for a less serious illness might be able to walk right in. And anyone convicted of violating this process, or attempting to go around the system, would have been fined as much as five thousand dollars and been sentenced to five years in jail. And that includes both doctor and patient.

To make the point a little better, let me give you a personal example of how this would have played out for me. At the time this plan was being debated in Washington, I had a close personal friend who was a congressman and who basically agreed with the plan and was a vocal supporter. He was a good personal friend, and I even stayed with him a few times when I was traveling back and forth to DC on business. He was a liberal, but I admired him because he was consistent, and he sincerely believed in the principles he supported. Unlike a lot of people on that side, he did his homework and could hold his own in any debate.

At one point in her life, my oldest daughter, as an infant, had a structural problem in one leg that forced her foot inward, slightly pigeon-toed. It was easily correctable with orthopedic shoes. It took one hour of a doctor's time to fix it, and the shoes cost five hundred dollars. Under Hillary's plan, she would never have gotten those shoes. It wouldn't have been a priority, and as a result, my lovely daughter would have been crippled as an adult. On one occasion I described the situation to my friend, the congressman, at one of our local forums. He openly admitted that those shoes would never have been available through Hillary Care.

But that was OK, he said. She still would have been able to walk. That comment really got to me. I replied that she wouldn't have been able to run track or play soccer, to be a cheerleader in school, or to pursue her interest in dance. His response was straight down the party line: "This is how you manage health care," he said. "The major needs get attention and the minor needs do not." But then he said that if anyone tried to go around the system, or took any sort of action not approved by the system to get some doctor to prescribe my daughter's corrective shoes, it would be a five-thousand-dollar fine and five years in jail. Do you think for a minute that the people of Oklahoma didn't see the problem with that kind of thinking?

THE DEMAND FOR FREEDOM

But it gets worse. There have been many news stories in recent months about the "health tourists" from Great Britain and other European countries going overseas for medical treatment. According to a recent report in the *London Sunday Telegraph*, as many as seventy thousand British citizens who are already taxpaying participants in the government's mandatory National Health Service (NHS) are traveling to countries such as Hungary, Turkey, Germany, Malaysia, Poland, and Spain for diagnosis and treatment they've been refused in their own country. And in most cases they're paying for it out of their own pockets. An NHS report estimated that as many as two hundred thousand British citizens will likely leave the country for treatment abroad by the year 2010.[2]

When I mentioned the possibility of seeking alternative treatments at my own expense, the liberal advocates of Hillary Care went so far as to suggest that if I left the country for the simple procedure my daughter required, I would be fined. Unfortunately, there's still an ongoing debate about such things today. According to one advocate of these programs, if any American citizen leaves the country to live abroad, they would have to forfeit 30 percent of their assets to the government, because it was government, they claim, that allowed them to earn the money.

To a Socialist, all assets are owned by the government. What you get to keep is a gift from the state. But this is not the way the people of this country have ever thought about it. For anyone who believes in freedom, government is only there to protect your rights and privileges. That's why we say that law enforcement, the military, basic infrastructure, and public services such as clean water, sewage and waste pickup are the only necessary functions of the state. The assets we earn, accumulate, inherit, or achieve by any other means belong to us, and what we give to government in the form of taxes belongs to us as well, not to them.

I can only say thank goodness Hillary's health-care plan didn't pass. My daughter got the shoes she needed. That was our family's decision. She did, in fact, go on to play soccer. She was a cheerleader and pom in school, and she was a wonderful dancer and performer. And the reason was because of the innovation that, for the moment at least, sets this country apart from all those who have chosen the Socialist, big-government alternative, which is that we are a free and independent-minded people who have the tenacity to do things for ourselves. We're freedom-loving people to the depths of our being.

But all of this brings to mind another story that relates to the above. It involves testimony before Congress at about the same time the health-care debates were under way in Washington. At one point there was another hearing in the Capitol, in which one of the witnesses was a Russian farmer who was discussing how deplorable the Soviet system had been during his whole life and how the burdens of Communism were destroying his people. I related to him because he spoke, at one point, about shoes for his children in a somewhat different context.

He told the committee he had a small herd of cattle that he managed for the state. He owned nothing and enjoyed no benefits from his labor other than the standardized pay he received from the state. One of the most moving parts of his testimony was when he spoke about one particularly difficult calving birth. The mother cow had gone into labor in the early evening, but she didn't give birth right away. Then again at midnight it appeared that she might deliver her calf, so the farmer went out to help it along. The temperature was below zero and it was raining. But, once again, it was false labor.

At 3:00 in the morning, the mother cow was moaning in the barn and obviously required assistance. But when he was saying all these things, the Russian farmer made the point that whether the calf was born alive or not didn't make a bit of difference to someone at his pay grade. He didn't get to choose how he spent his money or whether or not to buy shoes for his children; all such choices were made for him by the state. But I will never forget what he said next: "I love my children and I want them to have shoes, but when it makes no difference, how many farmers do you think will get up at 3:00 in the morning to help deliver a calf?"

This man wasn't interested in the money for himself; he wanted to buy shoes for his children. But by robbing him and his fellow countrymen of their incentive, they had been stripped of their dignity and reduced to the level of uncaring machines. Without freedom, as Ronald Reagan had said, there is no opportunity, and without opportunity our children will have no future. In this case, the Russian farmer's humane instincts to aid a suffering animal were overcome by the futility of his situation.

FREEDOM OF OPPORTUNITY

These and similar experiences in Socialist countries have helped me to understand just how important this concept of freedom can be for the future of our children. On one occasion, when I served as counsel to the National Tax Limitation Committee, working closely with the distinguished economist Milton Friedman, I invited him to come to Oklahoma for a fund-raising dinner. I wanted him to speak about the importance of free enterprise and the capitalist system in America. No one does it better, and the first event would be at Oklahoma Christian College, in Edmond, Oklahoma, which was a great forum for a discussion on free enterprise.

After being introduced, Dr. Friedman stood up, and his first remark was, "What's a Jew boy like me doing speaking at a Christian college?" As soon as he said those words, I sank down in my chair. I thought, "Oh, my goodness! I've offended him and made a huge mistake." But sensing my discomfort, Dr. Friedman turned around and looked at me and said, "Relax, Marc; I'm just making a point." Then he turned back to the microphone and said, "The reason a Jew boy like me is speaking at a Christian college is because we both believe in, and absolutely depend upon, freedom." At that point, he went into his prepared remarks, and that speech stands out in my mind to this day as one of the best I've ever heard.

Without economic freedom, he said, there is no freedom. Unless we have the autonomy to earn, invest, and take risks with our own financial resources, we will never be anything more than slaves to the state. And when we are slaves to the state, there is no opportunity for growth and no religious freedom for anyone. It doesn't matter whether you're a Jew, a Christian, or a Muslim. Without freedom you cannot worship as you please.

All our hopes, dreams, ambitions, and even our human potential depend upon an environment of freedom. We ought to remember that the Boston Tea Party, which was one of the first acts of rebellion that led to the American Revolution, was primarily a protest for economic freedom. The colonists were sick and tired of suffering under the demands of the English king. Yes, it was about "taxation without representation." But representation demands a democratic system; freedom and democracy go hand in hand. And the spark that ignited the War of Independence was, from the first, the citizens' demand for economic freedom.

Small-business owners work an average of seventy hours per week. They use their own capital and take great risks. They struggle for an average of five years before reaching any level of success. But then, what does a small-business owner want? Why do they go into business for themselves? NFIB conducted a major nationwide study with Gary Lawrence of Lawrence Research to get to the bottom of that very question. You might have thought that the number-one reason was to make money, or to pursue a certain career, or to locate in a certain area.

It turns out the number-one reason that a small-business owner goes into business for himself is freedom—the opportunity to take risks, the opportunity to make his own decisions, the opportunity to use his talents as he sees fit. Simply put, to be free. The second reason is to spend more time with his family. Yes, business owners work long hours, but they get to decide when they work, and they give quality time to their families. The fastest growing sector of small-business owners today is women. They give the same reasons: control of their own time and the freedom to be with family. These are the people whom we should trust to tell us what we need for social services. They want to do what's right by their employees, who, in turn, trust them for it. We should trust individuals, not regulations in the hands of bureaucrats who favor managed growth and Europeanization.

You may find it interesting that another little-publicized characteristic of small-business owners in this country is that a sizable majority of them are self-defined evangelical, born-again Christians. They see freedom and opportunity as a moral obligation that must be maintained for our children's future. Of course, it's perfectly fine and appropriate that half the population works for big business or government. Both work together for a strong American economy. But we should never take away the right of people to make decisions for themselves freely and without restraint when it involves the members of their own families about their economic prosperity.

Those who favor the big government-managed economy paradigm wouldn't agree with most of the things I've been saying in these pages. They have another very different agenda, and they tend to think in long-range theoretical terms about issues on a much grander scale. That's why they're less concerned with a pair of shoes or the birth of a calf in the middle of the night. That's why they prefer to talk about the big picture, the global options, and the macro scale of the coming globalized economy. And that's why we must do everything we can think of to keep these people away from the seat of power.

Chapter 8

WHERE LIBERTY IS DENIED

*I predict future happiness for Americans if they can
prevent the government from wasting the labors of the
people under the pretense of taking care of them.[1]*

—THOMAS JEFFERSON

In the 1990s, the Disney Corporation conducted an international research project to determine how the citizens of
various nations and cultures define *happiness*. They found
that different cultures define happiness in surprisingly different ways. In the West, happiness tends to be escapism into
pleasure. When asked what makes them happiest, Americans
speak most often about having fun, being with friends, listen-
ing to their favorite music, and especially going to beautiful or
exotic places.

That is, of course, just what Disney likes to hear, since, as
Walt Disney insisted, "We are basically selling happiness."[2]
But in many parts of the world today, having fun is out of
the question. In some places just knowing that you'll be able
to eat a meal is happiness. In one country it may be having

a job, any job. In another country, it might be the security of knowing they'll be able to feed their children. And in too many countries to name, happiness is freedom from the peering eyes of the state and the ability to live freely and raise a family.

When you enter the Magic Kingdom, you'll find that it's devoid of everything possible that reminds you of the real world. The Disney theme parks and their personnel have made every effort to provide an environment with as little stress as possible. The images and experiences visitors have during their stay are custom designed to generate happiness and an escape from reality. Now that Disney is building its parks around the world, it may be interesting to see how they apply what they've learned from their study.

I found the Disney report fascinating. It's amazing how differently people responded to the questions. What the citizens of one country simply took for granted was often what the citizens of some other countries would have considered the ultimate joy. But the common bond between all countries and cultures had something to do with children and family—like wanting to spend more time with their children, or having children at all. For some it was having their children live with them. But all of them hoped for a better life for their children than the one they'd had, which I believe is a universal desire.

This focus on the importance of family also turns out to be equally common in countries going through political turmoil. Wherever I've traveled on political and diplomatic missions in Central and Eastern Europe, I've always made it a priority to learn as much as I could about the local culture and customs. I usually assumed the problems I'd been engaged to address would be something of national or regional concern—these were revolutionary times, after all—but, in fact, I always found that there were also personal, family, and community issues that were every bit as important as the political concerns.

FORMING A NEW NATION

In 1988 and 1989, the Eastern European nation of Bulgaria attempted to shake itself free from the yoke of Communist oppression. Communism had been forced on the country in 1949, following World War II and the creation of the iron curtain. Forty years later, an independence movement was sweeping Eastern Europe. The reform movement in Bulgaria was led by Dr. Zhelyu Zhelev, a scholar and fine artist who was elected president in August 1990 with the promise that he would help his country establish a parliamentary democracy similar to those in the West.

International observers were engaged to oversee the process and advise the leaders of the freedom movement on strategy, but they also needed legal counsel and assistance in drafting a new constitution. I was approached by my colleagues at the Krieble Institute about taking the assignment, but even before I accepted it, the Bulgarian ambassador in Washington called and requested an impromptu meeting, and it sounded urgent. All I knew about Bulgaria at the time was that it was a mysterious country behind the iron curtain. Little did I know that I was about to begin a trek that would show me just how similar people around the world can be when it comes to freedom and the hope of making a better life for their children.

When I arrived at the ambassador's residence in Washington, I couldn't help feeling like I was in an Addams family movie. It was a dark and foreboding building, an eighteenth-century mansion with big iron knockers on the door. My appointment was at 5:00 p.m. and the sun was already setting. When I knocked on the door I could hear footsteps in the distance. The door opened slowly with a creak, and I half expected Lurch to greet me. The man at the door was dressed like a butler, very formal in his manner but unaware of my appointment. He apologized but told me there must be some mistake. It was after hours. I had no formal invitation or letter from the ambassador; therefore, I must leave immediately.

As I peered over his shoulder, I could see past the door to a long flight of steps that looked like the elegant staircase in the final scene of *Gone With the Wind*. As I was about to depart, thinking there must have been some mistake, a voice rang out from the top of the stairs, yelling for me to wait and asking the butler who was at the door. The official asked me to wait and left me for a minute or so. When he came back, he simply waved his arm toward the bottom of the staircase.

The voice had been the ambassador's. He told me it was an emergency meeting. He escorted me to his study and got right to the matter at hand. He handed me a scroll that was rolled up on both ends and said, "This is the current draft of the new constitution of the Republic of Bulgaria. I need you to look at this and see if you can tell me what's wrong with it." I thought he wanted me to take it and write a memo with my analysis. But he said, "No, no, no! Look at it now!" I said, "You want me to read this right now?"

It was a lengthy document and hard to handle, but as I unrolled it he directed me to a particular passage. He said, "Start here, please. The flaw will jump off the page at you." Sure enough, it did. In the upper left-hand corner of the document, the drafters had copied the due process clause of the United States Constitution in reference: "All citizens have equal protection under the law, regardless of race, creed, color, or sex." But then, in a column to the right were changes to the document the framers back in Bulgaria intended to make. This time the due process statement said, "Every citizen has equal protection under the law regardless of race, creed, color, or sex, except the Turks." I looked up at the ambassador and said, "OK, I get it."

The ambassador was anything but what I had expected. He certainly wasn't from the Addams family. He was a young, articulate, and worthy patriot of Bulgaria. He cared about his country and its citizens. He told me, "Mr. Nuttle, you have to go to the constitutional convention and speak to them about this. I will make the arrangements, but you must get that clause out of the document." Of course he was right. You can't deny certain groups the right of due process. The Western legal system would never recognize such a constitution, and it would cause endless tension between the United States and Bulgaria.

I accepted the assignment, and before long I was on my way to Eastern Europe. When I arrived in the capital city of Sofia, I was met by a government official and taken directly from the airport to a meeting of the constitutional convention. Sofia, I discovered, is a beautiful old city, with ancient squares, cobblestone streets, and rugged but handsome medieval buildings. The convention was taking place in an old Shakespearean theater. We entered through a side door and walked down a long hallway used primarily by the actors. It was like walking into an arena. I was introduced to the convention as an expert on democracy and constitutional law. A bit of a stretch, perhaps, but it was enough to insure they would pay attention to my remarks.

LOOKING TO THE FUTURE

When I walked out onto the stage, I was taken aback. It was a very small stage and the audience was very close, sitting high on top of each other as if on ladders. I was used to theaters where the seats were barely raised and there was a lot more distance to the back row. There were several rows of seating, and the top row was no more than thirty feet from the stage. Most of the participants were dressed in traditional Bulgarian clothing; some were in suits, and many were in robes, representing various religious sects. Several were from the military.

I introduced myself and my purpose and said that my motivation was simply to bring forth some ideas for discussion. I argued that exempting the Turks was unacceptable because either all are equal under the law or none would be protected by the law. As ancient as the cultural conflict had been between the Turks and Bulgarians, citizens of Turkish descent had to be part of society just like everyone else. As I spoke, I could hear grumblings from several delegates; some began pounding their desks, yelling at each other and at me. As I was watching the commotion, I said there could be no compromise on this point. Their new constitution would not survive with such an overt discriminatory clause.

As I was making my point, a young man sitting on the front row stood up, climbed onto the stage, and began walking straight toward me. He didn't seem threatening, but it was strange that he would be walking onto the stage in that manner. I continued speaking, but when he walked past me, he whispered in my ear, "Keep it up. You're doing fine. You have more support than you realize." Then he kept on walking and exited through the side door through which I had entered.

Later in my visit, I found out who he was. His name was Christo Ivanov, and he was part of the freedom movement. Over the next few hours, I spoke to the general session and various side meetings, little realizing how important this issue would be for the independence movement. With only a few weeks to go until the referendum, we were running behind. Current polling showed the Communists had 49 percent of the vote and the Freedom Party had 41 percent. The Communists had done a good job convincing the people they would lose their pensions and food rations if they voted for freedom, so we had some ground to cover. Fear is a powerful weapon, but the promise of freedom is more persuasive.

I learned that the Turks lived primarily in an enclave in Southeast Bulgaria and represented about 10 percent of the population. They ran their own affairs in their own area of the country. The 41 percent number in the polls reflected only Bulgarian opinion and didn't include the Turks. After discovering that, I went to the leaders and said, "We need to get the Turks to support the constitutional reform, but I can't approach them with any logical propositions if they're excluded from the reforms. If you want the Turks to support the referendum, we'll have to make another push to eliminate the discriminatory language from the draft."

I got permission from the president to call a meeting, so we invited the Turkish leaders to Sofia to discuss the situation. I was honest with them. I told them exactly where things stood, and I said I needed their support for the referendum. In exchange, we would make sure the Turks were granted due process rights as equals under the law. When I said that, the Turkish leader pushed back from the table and stared at me. I've often wondered what he was thinking. The first thing he said was, "Why should we trust you?" I responded as a lawyer and said, "You'll see the draft before it goes to a vote." But that wasn't what he meant. He wanted to know if the Bulgarians would honor the new language after they put it in.

I said, "Have you had more rights under the Communists?" His answer was quick, "No." So I told him what James Madison said in the Federalist Papers, that the nation would be stronger under a Federalist government where each faction could watch the others to make sure their rights would be protected. Then I said, "You can either stay with the past, where you know you have no rights, or you can take a chance that in the future your children will have greater opportunity. But even if you take this chance and it fails, how are you any worse off?"

The Turkish delegation retired into executive session for a period of time. When they came back, they had a few questions about restrictions in the constitution as far as it related to the Turkish population. I assured them the constitution would protect all citizens equally. They looked at each other, then they looked at me, but, in fact, they had already made their decision. The leader stood up and said, "We'll take a chance on the future." I smiled and said, "Done." When I reported back to the president's offices, I told the reform leaders they now had the leverage they needed. The constitutional delegation could either include the Turks or there would be no constitution. Within a few days, the document was redrafted with the discriminatory language taken out.

DISMANTLING A TYRANNY

I was delighted to know we had accomplished our mission. We had helped the reformers produce a document that would guarantee more freedom for the Bulgarian people and help them establish a real democratic system. But I soon discovered that my enthusiasm was somewhat premature. Not everyone in the country, it turned out, was convinced that the new democratic reforms were realistic or safe. I also learned that the young man who had spoken to me on the stage that first day, Christo Ivanov, happened to be the chief of staff for President Zhelev, and he wanted to know if I would be willing to take on another mission.

Christo had been given the responsibility of planning and conducting the constitutional referendum. If the measure passed by a majority vote, the new reforms would establish the new constitution as the foundation of the new democratic state. But that might not be as easy as it sounded at first since most of the citizens had no recollection of life before Communism, and many had questions the reformers had not been able to resolve. In addition, dissident factions were stirring up trouble, trying to dismantle the whole process.

When I toured the cities of Bulgaria, I could see the damage that Communism had done. The countryside was truly beautiful with rolling mountains, lush meadows, and magnificent rivers flowing down to the sea. Situated between the Danube River on the west and the Black Sea on the east, the towns and villages of Bulgaria had all seen better days, and the roads were often rough or impassable. Farmers who had been happy prior to 1949, owning and running their own farms, were now part of the collective farming system. Everywhere I went the people seemed sad and dispirited, and even their homes and workshops were depressing.

At one time Bulgaria had boasted a thriving agricultural economy, growing corn, wheat, tobacco, and sunflowers, and exporting attar of roses for the European perfume industry. But since 1949 the standard of living had deteriorated dramatically. Lack of freedom had oppressed them to the point of depression without hope. They had learned what they never asked to learn—that totalitarian control and the loss of basic freedoms were emotionally and morally crippling. Despite the promise of lifetime security and social order, the price of servitude to the almighty state had become unbearable.

Over several weeks, we debated the Communists in open forums and university lecture halls. At times it seemed as if every step forward was met with two or three steps in reverse, and I was constantly being forced to explain the most rudimentary democratic concepts. Even for those who believed that democracy was the right answer and that Communism was little more than a prison sentence, it was a struggle for them to imagine how different their lives would be in a free society. They desperately wanted freedom but, at the same time, feared the changes required.

In addition, the leaders of the freedom movement were concerned about overpromising to the public about how fast the improvements would take place. And they were especially concerned about the safety of the people who stood up to oppose the Communist leadership. During a debate at the University of Gabrovo in central Bulgaria, I challenged the Communist leaders to name anything they had achieved that had benefited the public or the families of the area since

1949. After they had stumbled around with lame excuses and obvious lies, I described the kinds of improvements they could expect under a free democratic system.

After the debate, one of the Communist Party leaders came to the stage and said to me, "Last year I could have had you shot for directly challenging me like that." My response was, "Isn't it amazing how quickly freedom can strip you of your moral authority to oppress these people?" The anger of such men who have lost their power was not something to take lightly, but that was the environment that faced Bulgarian families at the time.

One morning during the campaign, the chief finance minister asked me to meet with a group of local mayors who were concerned about the future stability of their villages. The Communists had threatened reprisals if they did not denounce the reform movement. They were worried for their families. I told him I didn't know what I could say to them. It was easy for me as an American who was born free to say, "It takes courage." But I agreed to meet with them at the reform party's headquarters in downtown Sofia, just off Ruski Square.

I couldn't have been more humbled by their presentation. There were five of them from five villages. They dressed up for me as best they could. They were in tattered tweed coats; two had no coats and apologized to me for their appearance. It was all I could do to maintain my composure. These men had been oppressed for forty years. They knew they were taking a chance in supporting the freedom movement. They were risking their lives, much as our own patriots had done two hundred years earlier, and making a sacrifice I could only imagine. I tried to explain to them how honored I was to be in their presence, but I can only hope that they understood how sincerely I meant what I said.

They told me the Communists controlled the villages by doling out hay for the cattle and milk for the children and families once a week on Mondays. The party leaders had come to them and said, "If you do not denounce the freedom movement, we will withhold the delivery of hay and milk. Your children and your cows will go hungry." So these men had come to me to ask for advice. The spokesman of the delegation was a slight man who exuded sincerity. His suit was clean but well worn, and he was holding his wool cap in one hand. He had learned English in school many years ago, he said, and had a strong Eastern European accent. But he spoke my language much better than I spoke his.

DISARMING AGGRESSORS

His message to me was clear enough. "We want freedom more than anything in the world. We are willing to pay any price to get it. The reason we are willing to do this is because we want our children to be free and to have more someday than we have now. We know that freedom promises a better future for the children. With the election coming, but still six weeks away, our concern is how will we survive for six more weeks? What good is a better future for our children if they don't live long enough to enjoy it?"

At that moment, I was stumped. I didn't know much about the local customs and I didn't have an answer. We sat and stared at each other for what seemed an interminable amount of time but was probably no more than a minute or two. And then he spoke first. He looked up at me with tears in his eyes and said, "Maybe it's not fair for me to put this off on you. I love my children and I am willing to die for them. Let's discuss this among ourselves. We want to do what you're telling us to do. But we have many questions." I said, "Please, let me think about the problem for a few hours. I promise I'll get back to you." And so they left.

It was about 4:00 p.m. when we started that meeting. By the time we finished, the sun was already beginning to set beyond the hills to the west of the city. As I reflected on the words of those brave but uncertain farmers, I decided to take a walk around the main square of Sofia to collect my thoughts. I was still pondering the dilemma when I happened to meet a reporter for one of the American newspapers covering the upcoming elections. There was only one place in the entire city with outbound telephone lines for use by westerners. He said he had just used the telephone and was walking back to his hotel.

I was delighted to have someone to talk to about the situation in the villages, so I shared the mayor's story with him. Much to my surprise, he said, "I can help you with that. Give me the names of the mayors in the villages, and I will check every Monday afternoon so see whether the hay and milk has been delivered. If not, we'll make a story out of it. That's just the kind of thing I've come here to cover."

I couldn't have asked for a better answer. I couldn't be certain this plan would work, but at least we now had something to offer the farmers. So I went straight to the headquarters of the Communist Party and registered my complaint about their campaign tactics with the leader. He couldn't have been more arrogant and dismissive. He denied the allegations and said he couldn't be responsible for what people under his command did or did not do.

I said, "Really? Since when does the Communist Party give freedom to anyone?" I said, "Let me tell you what we're going to do. We're going to check those villages every Monday afternoon. The first time a delivery is missed, you personally are going to appear on the front page of every newspaper in the world. I will make you the poster child for corruption and political oppression." He looked at me and said, "You wouldn't do that." I said, "In a heartbeat!" And I added, "If you persecute these farmers, we'll follow up with any prosecution the law allows."

When I reported back to the mayors, I said, "Let's give it a couple of weeks." My newspaper reporter acquaintance did, in fact, check two or three of the villages for the next two weeks. The supplies were delivered. The threat was not carried out, and the mayors stayed the course. In addition, the Turks I'd spoken to earlier voted overwhelmingly to support the new constitution, which gave the reformers the needed margin of victory, and the referendum passed 51 percent to 49 percent. For me, that was an exhilarating experience, which showed once again the importance of determination and courage in the face of adversity.

Where liberty is denied, the people will eventually lose hope and sink into despair. The eighteenth-century English philosopher Thomas Hobbes had said that in times of war and political upheaval, the life of man is "solitary, poor, nasty, brutish, and short."[3] The Bulgarian people knew this to be true, but by God's grace, they found a way out.

BUILDING A DEMOCRACY

My next assignment took me to another political hot spot, this time inside the tempestuous region of Ukraine, which declared its independence from the former Soviet Union in 1991. At the time I went there the country was, like Bulgaria, planning to hold free elections to establish this former Russian territory as an independent nation-state. The new country would have a constitution, a parliament, and democratically elected officials.

Unlike Bulgaria, however, Ukraine had never been an independent country except for a brief period after the overthrow of the Russian czar. But I soon found out that this was an election with much more at stake than the independence of Ukraine. If the citizens were successful in seceding from the Soviet bloc and establishing themselves as a free country, the entire Soviet Union would be in jeopardy of breaking apart.

Ukraine had long been known as the breadbasket of Europe. It was a major provider of grains not only to the Soviet republics but also to Europe and other parts of the world. The Soviet economy was a failure in most respects, and that was one of the reasons the various republics were eager to go their own way. But it would not be so easy for Ukraine to avoid Russian interference since the Russians depended heavily on the agricultural products from that region. But into this picture comes Boris Yeltsin, who had once been a colleague and protégé of the Soviet leader Mikhail Gorbachev. Yeltsin was named head of the Communist Party in 1985 but was kicked out when he broke with Gorbachev after only two years.[4]

By 1989, Yeltsin made a comeback and was elected to the People's Congress. As soon as he built his network of loyal supporters, he resigned from the party and was elected president of Russia in May 1990. The following year he led the resistance against a coup by the Communist hard-liners and presided over the final collapse of the Soviet Union.[5]

Communism had shown its true colors. Central planning and totalitarian control had oppressed the people to the point of desperation. They were willing to sacrifice everything for a taste of independence and freedom. The Communist promise of giving up freedom for security was meaningless, and with the flow of information and images from the West, the people were aware that they had been lied to and cheated. While they were living hand to mouth in poverty and despair, the democratic nations of the West were prospering. Blue jeans, rock music, and American movies had given them grounds to question the perpetrators of their imprisonment, and the spirit of revolt was in the air.

As all these forces were coming into play, a Ukrainian nationalist group had sought help from the various agencies and democratic associations in Washington DC. Predictably, the United States State Department refused to get involved; the driving animus of the diplomatic establishment in Washington was for stability and predictability at any price. They didn't want the Soviet Union to come apart, because they feared what might come later. Some apparently argued, though not on the record, "Better the devil you know than the devil you don't."

At that point the friends of Ukraine in the international community had approached the Krieble Institute for assistance, and some of my congressional clients who knew of the work I had done previously in Eastern Europe recommended me for the job. My sponsor would be the National Endowment for Democracy (NED), which is a quasi governmental agency. The NED is a private, nonprofit, grant-making organization created in 1983 to help strengthen democratic institutions around the world. The organization is also nonpartisan, with prominent supporters in both of our major political parties, and a large and well-informed base of support. These would all prove to be valuable assets for the task at hand.

When I arrived in the Ukrainian capital of Kyiv I began immediately to evaluate the situation, but I didn't have any idea what I would encounter. I was picked up at the airport by John Hewko, an American whose parents were native Ukrainians. John was an international lawyer working in that part of the world. He spoke fluent Ukrainian, a language that had once been banned by the Russians, and he had tremendous insight into the customs, culture, and living conditions in that country. John is now the vice president of operations for the Millennium Challenge Corporation in Washington. He lived at that time with his wife, Marga, in a two-bedroom apartment in central Kyiv. Their home also served as the freedom movement's campaign headquarters. We had no other office space. To this day, I am beholden to Marga for what she put up with, with dozens of us camping out and conducting business from that small apartment.

My job was to evaluate the situation and advise my sponsors back in Washington on what was required to establish democracy in Ukraine. To make my recommendation, I would need to develop a campaign strategy and prepare a workable budget. There had never been elections in Ukraine before. There were no precincts, no voting lists, no registrations, no ballot boxes, and no history of how to create such things. Everything had to be designed and implemented from scratch. But with John Hewko's help, I wrote the plan and submitted it to my associates in the United States. I was not bashful about what the plan would cost.

We got the help we needed from the National Endowment for Democracy and Paul Weyrich of the Krieble Institute. A lot of the funding came from Ukrainians living abroad who wanted freedom for their country. We didn't lack for support in that regard. Twenty percent of the Ukrainian population was Russian. They were concentrated in the northeast corner closest to the Russian border. There was a threat of civil war if the election for independence was close. Without the overt support of the United States, I was concerned about the outcome.

There were no embassies in Kyiv. It wasn't a nation. But there was an American attaché in Moscow who represented the Ukrainian region, so I went to see him using my Krieble Institute and National Endowment for Democracy credentials. I was glad to discover that he was a good man, knowledgeable about the cultures and the politics of the region, and he believed that Ukrainian independence was very likely. I requested political support for the effort but, once again, the State Department chose to remain neutral—in deference, I believe, to Mikhail Gorbachev, who was still the Soviet premier at that time. I informed the office of the attaché of the work I had been doing and said I believed the vote for independence would pass, but I wasn't sure by how great a margin.

THE CRY OF THE HEART

Other Western nations supported the independence effort, however, and on one occasion I was asked by the Ukrainian president Leonid Kravchuk to meet with a delegation of Ukranian nationalists living abroad to tell them what they could do to help the effort. I remember that each of those expatriates knew exactly what they wanted after the election was successful. It was almost humorous. The Turks wanted trucking rights. The French wanted to print the new currency. The Italians and the Japanese wanted trade licenses and shipping rights in the Black Sea. The Germans wanted to establish the banking system and provide computer technology. And it seemed that every one of them was well prepared to make his case.

Suddenly I understood the purpose of the meeting. So when they asked me what I needed, I knew I had a few bargaining chips. There were six distinct political regions, or oblasts, in Ukraine. To conduct the elections, I would need automobiles and fuel for six weeks for our staff in those six areas. We would need computers to manage the elections. So when I laid out what I wanted, the Germans and French were quick to accept both of these responsibilities. I also needed supplies, materials, telecommunications systems, along with a good statistical analysis of the demographics in the six voting regions. All was provided.

When everything was settled, the German representative said to me, "So, Mr. Nuttle. What do you get out of this?" I smiled and said, "Good government." At that, they all stood up and thanked me for pulling things together. On his way out the door, the German representative paused briefly, then reached over and shook my hand and said, "Well, God bless you."

We were off to a good start, but a few weeks prior to the elections, Premier Gorbachev decided to take a stand. In a speech to the entire nation, he warned that there would be a price to pay for those republics seeking independence. He didn't define what that price would be, but he later sent Soviet tanks into the streets of Kyiv. People were frightened that this would turn into another disaster, like Czechoslovakia in 1956 when a popular uprising was put down with force. The elections were not called off and the tanks did not leave.

The general in charge of Ukrainian forces asked our team whether or not we believed that Gorbachev would give the order to fire. I said I didn't know, and I understood the responsibility on his shoulders. Millions of lives were at stake. He asked me to inquire of the United States government their opinion in this matter. So I went back to see the attaché in Moscow, and he was kind enough to receive me a second time. When I told him about the general's concern and his request for information about the potential for military reprisals by the Soviets, he offered to contact Washington and find out what he could.

To President George Herbert Walker Bush's everlasting credit, he reacted strongly to the Russians' saber rattling and denounced Gorbachev's move. He publicly told Gorbachev that if he gave the order to fire on the Ukranians, he would be ostracized by the West. Information was then given to me by the attaché in Moscow that they didn't believe Gorbachev would execute the order, but no one was entirely certain about that. My only option then was to give the general the information he'd requested and let him and President Kravchuk make the decision.

As we were putting our plans into operation and setting up the elections apparatus in the outlying districts, the colonel in charge of military operations for Kyiv called to ask if we could arrange a face-to-face meeting. This was the man who would have faced the brunt of the Soviet force if Gorbachev gave the order to attack. When I arrived at his offices, he had many questions about America, our way of life, and our democratic institutions. I answered all of them as best I could. Then, like the Bulgarian farmers, this man looked up at me with tears in his eyes and said, "If we do this, Mr. Nuttle, and if we stand by these elections, how long will it be before my children will have the same opportunities as your children?"

Again I was taken aback by the emotion. This was a hardened former Communist military colonel who was telling me that the only thing he really cared about was his children's future. I knew how serious a question it was, and I didn't want to mislead him. So I paused briefly, then said, "Not in your lifetime, Colonel. But maybe in your children's and your grandchildren's lifetime." When I had spoken those words, he pushed back from the table and looked at me again for what seemed an interminable length of time, and we just stared at each other. As he nodded his head, tears welled up in his eyes, and he said, "Then that is a worthy price to pay for their freedom."

So we went ahead with the elections. My colleagues Sal Russo and Tony Marsh produced a series of very effective TV ads under difficult circumstances. We actually put the Ukrainian general on television for one of the first political ads ever aired in that country. He encouraged the people to vote, even in the presence of Soviet soldiers and their tanks. And they did. Gorbachev did not issue the order to fire. The tanks withdrew. The independence referendum passed by almost 80 percent. Civil war was averted, and Ukraine became an independent nation. And soon thereafter, the Soviet Union collapsed.

Seeing how all these things played out, and hearing the heartfelt yearnings of those people for freedom, had a profound impact on my thinking. I have always felt strongly about the importance of our democratic institutions, which is why I chose this profession in the first place. I've spent the last thirty years trying to spread the word that freedom isn't free. But seeing the thirst for personal liberty and the right of self-determination up close and personal, on the ground in those impoverished countries, was a powerful reminder of what's really at stake when men and women cry out for freedom.

Chapter 9

OUT OF THE DARKNESS

Liberty lies in the hearts of men and women; when it dies there, no constitution, no law, no court can save it.[1]

—JUDGE LEARNED HAND, 1944

In an important essay about the undeniable passion for freedom within the human heart, called "The Tide in the Affairs of Men," Milton Friedman writes, "Nothing is inevitable about the course of history, however it may appear in retrospect. Because we live in a largely free society, we tend to forget how limited is the span of time and the part of the globe for which there has ever been anything like political freedom: the typical state of mankind is tyranny, servitude, and misery."[2]

Here again, Dr. Friedman goes right to the heart of the matter, which is that freedom is a rare and precious jewel in the history of nations. It is a treasure to be protected at all costs and handed down to the next generation with loving care. But there's no guarantee that will happen unless we understand the risks. One of the greatest dangers facing this nation today—especially for the younger generation that has never had to pay the price for freedom—is that we've never been forced to sacrifice for our liberty.

Very few of us have ever looked down the muzzle of a gun in the hands of a totalitarian zealot. Our children have never had to earn their bread by the sweat of their brow. In fact, a surprisingly large number of young people in this country have never left the nest and are still living at home with Mom and Dad, sometimes into their thirties and forties. This isn't to say that we don't have many bright, hard-working young people who care about all these things, but since the end of the Second World War, we've had it pretty good.

Most Americans have grown up far removed from those parts of the globe where freedom doesn't exist. We can't imagine going a day without a fast-food break or stopping at Starbucks for a double mocha latte. But most of the world has never known such luxuries. As my friend Dr. Friedman writes in his essay, "the typical state of mankind is tyranny, servitude, and misery." Most of the adventures that American young people have discovered in their pleasure-seeking lives generally happen in video games or at Disney World. How little they know about the suffering of those like the Bulgarians and Ukranians I described in the last chapter, or of the freedom fighters hiding beneath the forest canopies of East Africa I encountered on my most recent foray abroad.

For more than twenty years now, Sudan has been engaged in a civil war between the Islamic population in the North and the Christian and animist populations in the South. The North is Muslim, controlled by Middle Eastern interests. The South is supported primarily by the United States and Israel. The war has been raging in one form or another since the early 1980s, long before the world became aware of the genocide in Darfur. But thanks to the outcry from the Christian community, President

George W. Bush decided to get involved and used diplomatic pressure to broker a cease-fire.

The International Republican Institute (IRI), in cooperation with the U.S. State Department, had been working on a series of projects to train the southern rebels in the process of establishing a new government. In 2004 I was asked to join a team to meet with rebel leaders in Nairobi, Kenya, to discuss the strategies of nation building and to find out what sorts of resources and assistance we could provide. I was approached by my contacts in Washington and informed about the risky conditions in that part of the world, but I knew this was something I wanted to do. So I took the assignment.

FORESTS OF THE NIGHT

When I arrived in Nairobi, I had been traveling for thirty-six hours straight. There had been weather problems in the United States, and making connections to Kenya was a challenge. When I arrived at my hotel, the IRI and State Department officials told me, "There's good news and bad news. The good news is that the peace talks are on schedule, and the two-week window set aside for these projects is on course. The bad news is that we have to fly into the jungle to meet with the rebel leaders at their base, and we'll be leaving from the Nairobi airport in one hour."

I didn't even get to check into my room. We went straight downstairs, jumped on the transport vehicle, and headed back to the airport. From Nairobi we flew commercially to the northern border of Kenya into a rural airport on the Sudanese border. From there we had to take a chartered flight into the jungle. So the six of us on the diplomatic team jumped on an above-wing propeller plane loaded down with four fifty-gallon tanks of diesel fuel for the generators and other motorized equipment at the rebel camp, and we headed off into the sunset.

During the flight, I noticed that the pilot was speaking Ukrainian. I didn't understand much of what he said, but at one point I spoke to him in what little Ukrainian I remembered, and I could see it made him feel good. He told me he was a contract pilot for a United Nations relief agency, and his mission was to ferry people in and out of these remote villages. These pilots work eighteen months at a time in some of the roughest conditions on the earth.

We flew over the canopy until the pilot spotted an airstrip carved out of the jungle. Instead of just landing, he flew over it, then took the plane almost into a vertical stall before diving in for a quick landing. I yelled at him from the front seat, "What are you doing?" He said, "This is the way we approach these airstrips. It frustrates the efficiency of small arms fire." Hearing that, I looked back at my State Department counterpart and said, "Somehow you failed to mention that part!" He was a former special ops Ranger, so he was accustomed to these tactics. His quick reply was, "Don't worry. It'll be all right." I wasn't so sure about that, but I just nodded and hoped for the best.

From the airstrip we took a jeep to the rebel camp where we were to meet the leaders. They had been trying to set up some semblance of a government but not getting very far. My job was to discuss with them the mechanics of setting up essential institutions, including a federal reserve system, managing currency, and maintaining a central bank. Beyond that, I was to deal with the general structure of democratic institutions, political parties, and a parliamentary form of government. That first day in camp we took care of logistics and got acquainted with some of the leaders. Then, over the next couple of days I talked to them about all these things and answered their questions.

As we concluded our discussions one afternoon, the colonel in charge of rebel forces pulled me aside and said he had a few questions. We were standing under a large mimosa tree. This large, muscular man stood about six-feet, six-inches tall and was an imposing figure by any standard. But having been with him for a few days, I understood his desire for independence. He loved his people and believed that freedom was their only hope. As in Bulgaria and Ukraine, I didn't know the full story yet, but I understood the longing. He asked me, "Marc, when are you coming back?" I said, "Whenever the IRI or the State Department sends me back. I'm here on their authority." We talked about that for a minute, and then the full story came forth.

He said, "Look, Marc. I've been hiding under the canopy of southern Sudan for twenty years. The North has airplanes. We do not. If they find us in the open, they shoot us. My children have moved from camp to camp their entire lives. I don't want to go back under the canopy, and I don't want this way of life for my children." And, again, as in Bulgaria and Ukraine, this big man had tears in his eyes as he spoke those words. We stared at each other for a moment, and then he said, "Marc, I will do whatever is necessary to save my country's children. Please, we will pay any price. Show us how to take the next step."

All I could say to him was, "Sir, I will try." I genuinely meant what I said, but how could I help? All my knowledge and experience and compassion would never be enough to stop the injustice or defeat the tyranny that was bearing down on so many thousands of suffering and desperate people in Sudan.

We Americans live in a country that no longer has to face the question of survival. We occupy ourselves with trivial amusements and spend our waking hours searching for more and more ways to fill our leisure time, while millions are living on the edge of starvation in the forests of the night. How can we turn our backs on these people? We must do everything we can to end the tyranny. But there's another lesson here: we must never let this precious gift of liberty we take for granted slip through our fingers, or there will be no safe harbor for the world.

BEHIND THE BAMBOO CURTAIN

The types of change driving our anxiety about the future today are mostly forces that we did not create and cannot control. We can stand against them, but these forces aren't going away, regardless of how hard we may try to stop them. Our children look to us with angelic trust to give them a life in which they can attain the potential that God designed for them before they were born. But we can only satisfy that innocent plea if we remain dedicated to the proposition that freedom is not free and remember that the price of freedom will always be eternal vigilance.

The forces that concern us are diverse, disconnected, and complex, and they come against this country because we're the only ones, so far, who've successfully resisted their advance. One of the most salient challenges at the moment is our relations with China. These two countries are as different as any two cultures can be, and despite the current atmosphere of cooperation in trade relations, there is potential for serious division between our two countries at some point if political and diplomatic relations should ever weaken.

To understand Chinese culture, it helps to understand how Asian people look at time. Because of their long history, the Chinese people believe that no great questions can ever be answered in the present. What begins today is finished tomorrow. This generation understands that they're expected to carry on with whatever the prior generation has begun. This generation may have new ideas and may introduce changes along the way, but these things will always be in context or connection with the past. And whatever begins today will be tied to those who come tomorrow. To break this chain of continuity would be unthinkable.

China is the only country under total Communist control that is a member of the World Trade Organization. This is remarkable when you think about it. How can a Communist country that still believes in a command economy controlled by government be a member of a world trade organization that responds not to government but to the demands of the marketplace? The answer lies in what the Communist Chinese did when they took over mainland China in 1949.

The first thing the Communist leaders did was replace the republic established by Chiang Kai-shek with a Communist government. However, they didn't try to replace the feudal system that had been in place in the provinces for thousands of years. Instead, the warlords were given rank as generals, and the government replaced the emperor with a politburo, which is the Communist central committee. No matter how the warlords responded, the Communists would have won, but instead of doing battle with the old order, they brought them into the system.

Today the Chinese government manages the economy from the top down. It often seems this country is headed in that direction, but at least in principle the United States must do things differently. Congress passes a budget, personal income and corporate profits are taxed pursuant to the tax code, and government then dispenses funds and pays its debts from tax revenues. If the economy does not produce enough revenue to meet government's obligations, then government runs a deficit. The deficits are largely financed by treasury bills, which become an obligation of the government.

When the Chinese government establishes a budget, they tell each general what their share of the tax burden will be. Each general is responsible for paying the amount delegated to him. He makes his money back however he sees fit, by demanding payments from the people in the cities and towns of his region. This, incidentally, is why it's difficult to enforce intellectual property rights in that part of the world. If pirates copy a piece of software or an American movie and peddle it without paying royalties or fees of any kind, there will likely be protests from the copyright owners. But the generals in that region will never say a word, because they can tax those profits, and this is another way to recover their portion of the government's tax. Instead of being regulated by international law, he's simply operating by a system that allows him to recover his money in any way he sees fit.

FINDING COMMON GROUND

The major cities of Beijing, Shanghai, Nanjing, and Hong Kong have special relationships with the government. Shanghai has long been the financial capital of China. Nanjing is the ancient imperial capital. Hong Kong, which was the British provincial capital until 1997 under a one-hundred-year lease arrangement, is once again under Chinese control. Beijing is the current national capital. Each of these cities has government officials who administer federal policy, but they coordinate with the generals and their provincial commanders.

The more powerful generals lead their own military divisions. They actually buy and sell weapons with foreign countries. They don't control nuclear weapons, missile systems, or any sort of strategic weapons, but they do control a formidable array of combat arms. The government owns many Chinese corporations. These corporations, in turn, conduct business in the provinces and the major cities. The system is becoming more integrated, but businesses are not taxed from the bottom up, as in this country, but through this modernized feudal system.

But compare this to the way it was done in the former Soviet Union. When the Communists overthrew Czar Nicholas II and Vladimir Lenin seized power in 1917, the feudal system in Russia was already defunct. The Communists took over everything at the national and local levels and eliminated private property and took control of all the resources of the country. Communism was implemented from top to bottom. The Russians respected tradition but weren't bound to the past like their Chinese neighbors. So one of the first things the Marxists set out to do was disrupt and dismantle every sort of patrimony or generational connection.

Actually, this difference was explained to me by the Chinese themselves when I served as an advisor on international trade to the Chinese government from 1989 to 1994. A Chinese American confidant of mine emigrated to my home state of Oklahoma at that time and became a good friend. His father had been an executive of the Shanghai Stock Exchange in 1949 but was imprisoned by the Communists for being a capitalist. Still a child at that time, my friend and his family escaped to California.

It took seven years to get his father out of prison, but they managed to do it. It meant giving up all the assets they had acquired in their native country, but they knew that freedom was worth every penny. Ironically, approximately forty years later the government of China approached this special family, seeking advice on how to reopen the Shanghai Stock Exchange. This led to a consulting relationship and the sharing of important information with the United States government.

I was asked to take the assignment because of my experience in international trade and other government transactions. I had served on the Industrial Policy Advisory Committee for Trade and Policy Matters in the Reagan administration. This committee coordinated between the office of the U.S. Trade Ambassador (USTR) and the Department of Commerce. It was our job to review trade treaties being negotiated by the General Agreement on Tariff and Trade (GATT), which was the predecessor to the World Trade Organization (WTO).

The tragic Tiananmen Square massacre, in which thousands of pro-democracy demonstrators were killed, occurred on June 4, 1989. These demonstrations were led by labor activists, university students, and intellectuals seeking democratic reforms and the restoration of personal freedom in the People's Republic of China (PRC). The military crackdown was intense and dramatic, with some of the most shocking moments broadcast on televisions around the world. Depending on the source, the death toll ranged from a few hundred by government estimates, to four hundred to eight hundred by the *New York Times*, to as many as three thousand according to the live reports from Chinese students and the Chinese Red Cross.

Following the incident, several Western countries recalled their ambassadors in protest. This was something the Chinese government couldn't tolerate since they place a high premium on government-to-government contacts. They hold government officials in higher regard than businessmen and began searching for ways to reestablish the dialogue. This is how I became involved. During that time, there was no official contact at the ambassador level between China and the United States. I kept the United States government informed of my activities, and the State Department provided me with assistance when I needed it, and I believe the project benefited both governments. I was able to advise the Chinese government on reopening the stock exchange and, at the same time, to discuss issues important to both countries in reference to bilateral trade and international relations.

TESTING THE MARKETS

My host while I was in China was Zeng Qinghong, the chief of staff to President Jiang Zemin. My memos were circulated to Deng Xiaoping, who was one of the original elders who made the five-hundred-mile march across China in 1949, when Chiang Kai-shek was driven to Taiwan. The relationship developed to the point that the Chinese had more and more confidence in introducing me to high-ranking government officials. We didn't know then what we know now about the extent of the preparations the Chinese were making to enter the global free-market economy, but I had seen some of those processes in the works.

In 1975, Deng Xiaoping, who was the de facto head of government at that time, came to the conclusion that Communism doesn't work economically. He didn't give up on the theory, but to maintain growth and stability in the economy, he said the PRC would need to enter the world's competitive markets. To do this required three things: first, they had to establish a federal banking system that would allow money to be wired in and out of the country; second, they had to establish a currency that had an established exchange rate with other freely traded currencies; and, third, they had to provide for liquidity of investment by reopening the stock exchange.

The plan was brilliant and insightful in one important way: it was Deng's plan that before this transformation could take place, peasants had to be able to buy the basic staple of the country, in this case rice, at the current world price. In other words, with the money she had from the government, she paid the same price that the world paid for that basic food item. They tied the currency, the yuan, to the new Taiwan dollar and used this as their standard, and phased it in over a fifteen-year period. When these financial elements were implemented, the peasant in the countryside never had to experience price shock over the price of food.

This wasn't the case in the Soviet Union. They never made such plans. When the Soviet Union collapsed, there was no stock exchange, no federal banking system that allowed money to be wired in and out of the country, and the currency was never tied to any exchange rate with other currencies. As a result, the gold supply of the Soviet Union was virtually liquidated, and, more importantly, the typical peasant in that country paid as much as three thousand rubles for a loaf of bread. Needless to say, this was disastrous to the Soviet economy.

In my discussions with the Chinese government, I advised that they should reestablish the Shanghai Stock Exchange in coordination with the Hong Kong and Taipei exchanges, so that stock could be traded simultaneously on all three markets. At the time, Deng Xiaoping was still working for reunification of the PRC with the breakaway republic of Taiwan. The policy was then, as it is now, one China, two policies. Since that time, the Chinese have, in fact, absorbed Hong Kong, without the great disruptions of investments the international community had feared. They still struggle with democracy, but they allow for limited local control.

This problem of a free-enterprise system operating successfully under a Communist framework is a major source of concern. The Chinese fear the masses. They worry about revolt and unruliness getting out of hand, and this was no doubt what provoked the government's controversial retaliation against the demonstrators in 1989. There are also problems with people in the rural areas moving too quickly to the cities when there aren't enough jobs to support them. Yet, the Communist state has the same problems supporting rural areas that all countries do. Ten percent of the population of China today migrates without facilities to support them, much like European gypsies in the Middle Ages.

Any large migrating population can pose problems, but in China it must be addressed because the population is so vast. Ten percent of the Chinese population is 110 million people. Think what it would mean in the United States if 10 percent of the population was moving from site to site, camping out on open land or on the edges of our major cities. That would be more than 30 million people moving by caravan in large groups and living off the land.

IN PRACTICAL TERMS

When you begin to understand the history of China and the dedication of the Chinese people to tradition, you get a better sense of who they are and why they do things in such unique ways. After conducting our business discussions and attending long, formal state dinners, we would often relax over drinks to talk about world affairs. On one such occasion, the secretary of state of China asked how I would define freedom. I made my attempt by citing the Declaration of Independence and the Constitution and elaborating on the rule of law.

The secretary looked at me and said, "That's nice, Marc. But one of our definitions is 'the right not to starve to death.'" He told me that in 1962, 20 million Chinese starved to death, and the Communist government vowed that would never happen again. Then he asked me how I thought democracy was doing. Again, I tried to give what I thought was a sophisticated answer, and I said we were doing just fine. But no sooner than I had given my answer, he said, "Marc, it's a trick question. The correct answer is: It's too soon to tell!" We both laughed, and I did see his point. But he added, "When you live in a nation like China with more than six thousand years of history, your history in America of just slightly more than two hundred years is, well, it's just too soon to tell!"

I nodded and thanked him for his perspective, but I was also defiant in defending the history of democracy as the world's greatest experiment in government that served the people. America was living proof that democracy had created the greatest nation on the earth and was the model for all future governments. At risk of seeming overly nationalistic, I said that my own grandfather had fought in World War I and my father in World War II for freedom, and that I was as committed, generationally, to the concept of individual liberty and limited government as he was to China's six-thousand-year history.

It was a friendly scuffle and neither of us went away angry, but it was eye-opening to see how differently our two peoples view the world. The challenge for the Chinese was how to enter a world market for free enterprise and how to conduct a peaceful transition for the benefit of their people. The United States was born through a revolution demanding economic freedom and then democracy. I couldn't help but think of Alexis de Tocqueville's provocative comment in *Democracy in America* where he wondered how democracy would fare when the people discovered they could demand things from the public treasury, and he wondered whether democracy would be able to handle that possibility any better than the kings of Europe.

My relationships with the Chinese officials developed over time, to the point that I was asked to meet with the new director of national security for China, Jai Chun Wang, to answer his questions about Western expectations. When I informed my White House contacts that I had been asked to meet this important man, they brought me in for a briefing. It turned out the new director of security wasn't just new, he was brand-new.

After Tiananmen Square, several cabinet-level officials had been dismissed or reassigned. The office of security had been reorganized, and Jai was the first secretary of the new structure. At the White House briefing, I was given a list of questions to ask the Chinese. The White House officials were excited enough about my relationship with the Chinese leaders that they presented me with an organizational chart of the Chinese government as best they knew it prior to the Tiananmen Square debacle.

The chart unfolded into a document about two feet by three feet in size. I looked at it and said, "You expect the national security director of China to go over this chart with me?" They said, "Yes, if you get a chance, that would be great. And, by the way, since no westerner has ever seen this guy, Jai, how about seeing if you can get your picture taken with him?" I said, "Right! Who do you think I am, James Bond?" Most of these guys were pretty matter-of-fact and didn't really see the humor in that remark. But I concluded that no one really expected anything much to come of that trip.

DINNER IN BEIJING

As soon as I arrived back in Beijing, I was invited to stay at the official Chinese government guesthouse. I believe I was the first nonelected, non–State Department official to stay there. During the visit I was told I would be meeting with Jai, and he would appreciate my advice on dealing with the Western press and how I assessed the world's image of China. I was surprised when they said this because I had been very blunt about how the world viewed them after Tiananmen Square. I said they were considered to be a rogue state in most of the world. Maybe it was my honesty, or perhaps they felt I wasn't rendering a personal opinion. But they kept inviting me back and moving me into higher- and higher-level meetings.

The dinner was set with Minister Jai, and it would be held in the Great Hall of the People, which is used as the Chinese parliament building on the western edge of Tiananmen Square. The hall seats five thousand people, but on this occasion we would be seated at the only table in the room. There were ten of us at a large round table situated in the center of the hall. When the waiters came in with each course, it seemed to take fifteen minutes or more for them just to walk from the kitchen to our table. This was Minister Jai's first ever meeting with a non-Chinese nationalist. To be meeting with someone from the West, who could later criticize the officials, was a daunting process for him. You could have cut the tension with a knife.

I was seated to the minister's right. The delegation included members of the politburo and members of the executive committee of the Chinese Communist Party. The agenda for discussion included several topics, including trade and economic development, as well as questions about diplomacy and China's relationships with the West. But the evening wasn't going very well. Minister Jai was very stiff and overly cautious. Other than the honor of having dinner in the Great Hall, and in such a beautiful setting, I concluded that the evening wasn't likely to be very productive.

Nevertheless, I decided to take a chance. Family and history are important to the Chinese, so I thought I might explore that subject with these stern officials to see if they cared about their children as much as I care for my own. So I turned toward the minister and mentioned that I had seen his biography, which told about his background and mentioned his family. I said, "Minister Jai, I notice that you have a sixteen-year-old son." He nodded politely and said, "Yes." I said, "I have a fifteen-year-old daughter." At that point he looked at me quizzically, as if to say, "What's your point?" I smiled and said, "My question to you is, does your sixteen-year-old son think you're as stupid as my fifteen-year-old daughter thinks I am?"

He started to smile. Then he could restrain himself no longer. He laughed out loud and shot a piece of rice across the table like a missile, which hit the dignitary across from him on the forehead. Then he turned to me and said, "Mr. Nuttle, I am responsible for the internal and external security of 1.2 billion people. I am the combination of your CIA director, FBI director, and national security advisor, all in one. And my son literally doesn't know how I accomplish putting on my pants in the morning!"

At that moment, everyone at that table began to laugh, and the tension in the room melted away immediately. Suddenly we had a common denominator to which we could both relate— our children. He loved his son as much as I loved my daughter. And all that he was doing, from his point of view, was enhancing his son's opportunities for the future. Over the course of the dinner, conversation flowed freely. The minister would touch my arm or grab my shoulder as he told jokes. This is highly unusual for Chinese dignitaries; they don't usually touch in that manner.

As the evening wore on and we were becoming friendlier and friendlier, I said, "By the way, I have this chart that the United States government gave me. It's incomplete, and I wondered if you could fill in some of the blanks." He looked at me curiously and said, "What is it?" I said, "It is an organizational chart of the Chinese government." He said, "Let me see it." I got it out and unfolded it on the table. He held it up and started looking at it. Then he turned to me and said, "You mean this is the best the United States government can do?"

Then he started laughing. He pointed at the chart and said, "Well, this guy is dead. This guy is under house arrest..." and he went on that way for some time, pointing to other parts of the chart, "This post has been terminated," and so on. Before long he took the chart and laid it out on the table and said, "This is going to take a while." As we continued our discussions, he would pause and write on the chart as he thought of something he needed to correct, and he completely reorganized the layout. When dinner was finished and we were ready to leave, I said, "Minister Jai, I just have one more request. I need your picture." He thought that was a great idea, so we took a picture of Jai holding the chart.

When I got back to Washington to debrief my contacts, I pulled out the chart and the picture, and they just passed it on to the people who are responsible for such information without giving the matter a second thought. But before I left the White House, the officials who reviewed the document came running into the room, and said, "Where did you get this? How did you get this chart and this picture?" I just looked at them and said, "You got kids?" I didn't take time to explain, but I could see they were thrilled to have those documents.

China is still a mysterious country, difficult for most of us to get our minds around. They are not easy to work with and are not acclimated to the Western way of doing business. Recently the government of China has been restricting access to ships entering Hong Kong harbor, and they're requiring background checks on reporters covering the Olympics this year in Beijing. Things are more open than ever, but they haven't completely let go.

The Chinese still don't feel comfortable trusting people to be innovative in solving their own problems. The only life most people in that country can remember involves government control and regulation over every aspect of their lives. They're very intelligent people, but they're not very good at thinking, as we say, "out of the box." But there's reason to hope that one day soon, as the frequency of their contacts with the West increases, they may come to understand and appreciate the benefits of freedom. That would be a blessing for us and a giant leap out of the darkness for them.

Chapter 10

WORLD FORCES OF CHANGE

Freedom and liberty lose out by default because good people are not vigilant.[1]
—ARCHBISHOP DESMOND TUTU

When Ronald Reagan awakened this nation to the threats we faced from enemies foreign and domestic a generation ago, we listened, we reacted, and a movement was born. At the time we were mired in a hostile stalemate with the Soviet Union. Fears of a nuclear holocaust were being stirred up by saber rattlers on both sides of the Atlantic, and some of our own leaders were calling for compromise and lowering our defenses. But the American people refused to let down our guard. We confronted the forces of tyranny, and at the end of an epic struggle, President Reagan demanded that Soviet Premier Mikhail Gorbachev tear down that hideous wall that held half of Europe in bondage. Politicians and pundits accused the president of merely provoking the Soviets, but today the wisdom of that challenge is there for everyone to see.

When the Berlin wall came down in 1989, it was a great day for freedom-loving people everywhere. But today we're faced with a new set of circumstances and a very different political environment. In this first decade of a new century, we're being asked to deal with forces of unprecedented complexity and diversity—not only the dangers of terrorism and Islamic fascism but also new forces and problems that will raise questions the men of that earlier generation could never have imagined. Our moral imperatives are still the same—we understand the need to preserve our way of life—but how will we deal with problems posed by the Internet, global communications, the rise of nonstate states, and other issues that will test our resolve and determine where we stand a generation from now?

Perhaps most critical among these forces of change is the ongoing hostility between Arabs and Jews and the battle of wits taking place all across the Middle East today. Of all that has been written or said about this ancient theater of conflict, nothing is more telling than the observation that Jerusalem is the center of the conflict between Jews, Muslims, and Christians in the region, because all three of these historic monotheistic religions claim that city as a sacred place at the heart of their faith. And to this I would add one other fact that often goes unnoticed, which is that Jerusalem is not just a holy city for three major religions, but that all three of them claim Abraham's rock as an essential part of their identity. In the end, I believe, this is why the Mideast peace process has been so intractable for so long.

Abraham's rock, which stands atop the Temple Mount, is the place where God told Abraham to sacrifice his son Isaac. As recorded in Genesis 22, Abraham was obedient to the call, but upon demonstrating his obedience, God gave him a ram caught in a thicket to use as a substitute. Centuries later, after A.D. 661, a mosque was built at the site, and Muslim tradition holds that the Prophet Muhammad ascended to heaven from this place to receive instructions from Allah. The Dome of the Rock is now considered the third holiest site of the Islamic religion, after Mecca and Medina. There is a large indention in the rock that some Muslims believe to be the footprint of the angel Gabriel, who took Muhammad to heaven.

The blood feud between Arabs and Jews in Israel today revolves around the desire of both Muslims and Jews to control Abraham's rock. Only one religion can be correct about which of the descendants of Abraham is the true patriarch. Jews believe Isaac was the beloved son and heir of Abraham, while Muslims give that honor to Ishmael. In the eyes of Islam, Allah would never have allowed Abraham's rock to be controlled by any religion but Islam. This is why the peace accords brokered by President Clinton between Yasser Arafat and Israeli Prime Minister Ehud Barak inevitably failed.

Yasser Arafat was promised everything he had requested. The Temple Mount was to be controlled by a United Nations peacekeeping force, providing shared authority between Israel, Palestine, and Christian organizations in Israel. It would be a holy site that followers of the three great monotheistic religious could visit whenever they wished, and there would be respect and tolerance for each of them. But the peace process failed on this one point. Sharing authority with Israel would mean that it was possible that they had a legitimate claim to the holy city. And there could be no mutually agreeable solution to this dilemma.

Christians are less concerned with the Temple Mount, but we're associated with Abraham's rock through our relationship with Israel and our Judeo-Christian heritage. This is also why Christians are referred to as infidels by Muslims, because we believe in Jesus as the Son of God, who is of the line of David. Since World War II, United States foreign policy has consistently supported the State of Israel and its right to exist as an independent nation. This in itself brings the United States into conflict with the surrounding Arab nations.

As long as Israel exists and makes claims of historical precedent to the land of Palestine and the Temple Mount, there can be no peace in the Middle East, and the United States will be in conflict with Islamic extremists bent on forcing the Jews off the land and into the sea. Since the terrorist attacks in New York and Washington on September 11, 2001, no one needs to tell us that we're engaged in a bitter clash with Islamic extremists bent on our destruction, but the religious roots of this ancient feud are among the factors that will challenge our resolve in the years ahead. Each of us will need to know where we stand.

NONSTATE STATES

The fundamental challenge to the status of nation-states today is the emergence of a relatively new phenomenon called nonstate states. Nonstate states are organizations driven by religion, ethnicity, or economic interests. They're often structured around an emotion or need that transcends national boundaries. Their creed is tantamount to any constitution, government, or other authority. But the influence of the nonstate state is not limited to religion.

In the Pacific Rim, there is a Chinese nonstate state comprised of businessmen and investors who operate throughout China, Hong Kong, Taiwan, and Malaysia for the development of manufacturing and distribution of products around the world. These men recognize local law and customs, but sometimes they will maneuver around the law by using their own networks within traditional states. This type of organization is not without precedent.

During the Renaissance, the original investment-banking houses—often made up of brothers and family members from different countries—coordinated their activities to maximize profits. These organizations in and of themselves are not a threat to existing governments, but they do apply pressure to the United States economy, and that is yet another concern for the twenty-first century.[2]

Prior to the fall of the Soviet Union, the KGB (the Soviet secret police) had established a network of agents worldwide whose allegiance was to the KGB rather than to the country or any other organization. During the transition from the Soviet Union to the Russian Republic and the former Soviet republics, remnants of the KGB took part in activities that benefited the continued existence of that network, particularly in the distribution of raw resources. This is still a relatively small but significant concern for this country.

But perhaps the most visible nonstate states, and the ones with the most potential impact on our lives and the security of our families, are the various terrorist cells and religious organizations bound by their allegiance to their religion and their radical leaders rather than the state in which they reside. The ongoing conflicts between Shiite and Sunni Muslims still threaten the stability of Iraq and other Middle Eastern governments. And even though the militant forces of al Qaeda have been weakened by the United States forces and the recent military surge, the number of young Arabs willing to blow themselves up to make a political statement is a problem with no clear solution in sight.

As long as the United States is involved in supporting any of the existing governments in the Middle East, terrorism will continue to be a threat. Nonstate states do not believe in democracy or the peaceful transfer of power. These alliances between like-minded social, economic, and political interests are more akin to the tribal societies ruled by chieftains in ancient times. Control of territory meant survival. Nonstate states do not believe in trusting individuals to act in their own best interest. They believe that people must be controlled by those with the strength to lead. This too will pose a threat to our security.

COMBINED FORCES

All these forces are active today. They can't be avoided. We must deal with them. And there is one other force of great consequence that has the power to bring the entire world to a standstill: that force is oil. For the first time in history, a natural resource has returned full value to the country from which it has been extracted. In the past, natural resources were mined, shipped to a point of manufacture, value was added, and the wealth that was generated remained in the industrial state. The country where the raw material was actually found received little or no profit from the finished product. Today it's estimated that there is six trillion dollars of liquidity in the Middle East. This is an enormous amount of capital. How all this money will be applied for the world's benefit is not at all clear.

But there is a second force that derives from the same source. For the first time in history, the price of human labor is being paid to the state where the laborer resides. In medieval times, having access to cheap labor to work the land was a critical component of the economy. Landlords became wealthy off the sweat and toil of laborers who received minimal wages. But never before has cheap labor from one area of the world been used to dominate the flow of goods and services from one nation to other parts of the world. Japan accomplished this feat for a time after World War II, but never to the level that China is doing so today. It has been estimated that there may be as much as two trillion dollars of liquidity in China, and the primary source of that wealth is the enormous size of the Chinese workforce. How this will be managed to the world's benefit remains to be seen.

As mentioned before, the United States and Europe purchase 80 percent of the world's goods. In the process, both are becoming large debtor nations. Never before has such a disparity between liquidity and consumption existed. It's in the best interest of the Middle East and China to keep these Western nations functioning at full capacity. Otherwise, their customer base will disappear. China has the ability to develop a middle class over a period of years. It would be much more difficult for the Middle East to develop a large enough middle class to challenge the United States, Europe, or the Far East. But this could become a reality at some future date.

Another consequence of nonstate state pressure that is readily visible and important in this highly complex and increasingly dangerous world is the demand that the United States spend a substantial part of our tax dollars on military readiness and the deployment of forces around the world to defend our freedoms. Increased security at airports, deep-water ports, and other critical infrastructure will make the toll for costs that most nations do not have to bear a major concern in years ahead.

Among the more visible forces that affect how we live, the Internet provides accelerated competition for cheap labor and lower costs for goods worldwide. The challenge to traditional commerce is already a matter of concern, as in-store traffic decreases and online purchases increase. According to research from the comScore Networks, online sales in 2006 topped $102.1 billion, which was a 24 percent increase over 2005.[3] No doubt these numbers will continue to grow, but how will business respond? This nonstate state has the potential of threatening the United States economy if business fails to adapt to the changes and take advantage of this unique opportunity for expanding business in new ways.

The development of the Internet hasn't just changed the speed at which we communicate with each other; it has changed the way we manufacture, assemble, and distribute goods. Now that component parts of a product can be produced in different locations around the world and shipped to a central point of assembly, there is greater efficiency in manufacturing, greater economies of scale, and a greater need for high-speed communications of all kinds. But every step in this process represents some kind of risk—either commercial, technological, or legal—and we will need to be prepared for other changes in this process yet to come.

This combination of world forces will challenge our determination to preserve our great tradition of individual liberty. Some of these forces are daunting, but to retreat into a bunker of government protection will result not only in a lower standard of living but also in the one threat we must avoid at all costs for our children's future: life in a spiritual prison. Beyond choosing the right direction and making decisions about all these issues, we will need to be prepared to speak to others about our choices. The power of consensus can be an important weapon in our favor.

In deciding how you will participate in this process, the first requirement is to complete your own self-examination, as I laid it out in the early chapters. Psychologists tell us that people have definite personalities, such as passive or aggressive. It's natural and the way God made us, and there's not much we can do about it. That's why some employers require personality tests, so they can place their employees in positions that will maximize their strengths and minimize their weaknesses. The same holds true in political activity, and here are a couple of principles I've used in campaign management that may help you decide which approach is best for you.

THE 80/20 RULE

In any society—in this country and in any organization with a large number of people—20 percent lead and 80 percent follow. The 20 percent are the day-to-day activists who push and drive issues forward. The 80 percent are interested, they want information, and they will do varying degrees of work, but they will not take responsibility for the issues' advancement. There's nothing wrong with this formula. It's natural and the way God ordained it. It doesn't mean that the 20 percent are smarter or that the 80 percent are not carrying their share of the load. It's just the way each of us is wired.

The 80 percent are more than happy for the 20 percent to give them their options and allow them to make the final choices. We see this rule at work in many other ways in society. For example, about 20 to 25 percent is the average number of people who vote in political primaries. The 80 percent may be following the issues, but they're glad to accept the options given them through the primary process and the decisions made by the 20 percent.

It's about 20 percent of the population who follow the political talk shows on radio and television, who watch the Discovery Channel and read publications such as *U.S. News & World Report*, *TIME*, and *Newsweek*. The 80 percent will occasionally do these things, which raises these averages a little bit. But this pattern of active engagement with ideas and a persistent interest in what's happening around them will come, for the most part, from the 20 percent.

On national issues such as abortion, gays, gun control, federal deficits, balanced budget constitutional amendments, foreign policy, and the like, those in the 20 percent category who feel strongly about the issues will be at parity, split 10 percent to 10 percent. In other words, on abortion, the number of people fighting for it and the number of people defending against it will be roughly the same. This doesn't mean that the 80 percent will split evenly, however. The percentage of pro and con among this larger group depends on the issue.

The 80/20 rule is not something I discovered or that comes from new survey results. It's an established pattern identified by public policy analysts and sociologists over a long period of time. It reflects the way society responds to all the competing interests and activities going on around us and how individuals in our culture react to current events. But as you consider what this social dynamic means for you, the first thing you need to do is to ask yourself, am I wired as part of the 20 percent or the 80 percent? There's no wrong answer here. As Scripture assures us, all things work together for good for those who love God (Rom. 8:28). But once you've made this determination, you need to be a good citizen with the talents you've been given.

THE 30/30/30 RULE

Another rule that is important to understand when you're communicating your position to others, and therefore becoming an effective leader, is the 30/30/30 rule. It goes something like this: Thirty percent of the population gets up every morning, and the first thing they think is, "How am I going to get through this day without the help of government?" Or they may think, "I sure am glad we've got all these government programs; I just wish they would be expanded." Another 30 percent gets up every day and the first thing on their mind is, "How am I going to keep the government out of my business and personal affairs so that I can get through this day?"

The final 30 percent get up every morning and thinks about how they feel about their economic security. If they feel pretty good about it, they will lean with those who want less government. They seek opportunity, and they don't worry all that much about security. However, if they feel bad about their economic future, they will lean toward government programs as a backstop and lean toward the "security versus seeking" option. The remaining 10 percent of the population at any given time are disadvantaged, disabled, or otherwise disengaged.

These are average numbers, of course, but over decades of survey research probing the American psyche concerning their wants, needs, and fears, these numbers reflect the verifiable patterns of thought and behavior in this country. When Reagan was elected president in 1980, the anxiety level of the nation was reduced because the Iranian hostages came home and the country had confidence that President Reagan's strength of conviction would handle the Soviet threat. President Reagan brought new hope and optimism to the national debate, based on a strong image of America and his emphasis on economic growth through supply-side economics.

At that time, the 30 percent in the middle leaned right, toward the conservative values of the Reagan administration, because they felt good about their economic future. It's generally the movement of this middle 30 percent that swings national elections. In 1992, when James Carville coined the phrase, "It's the economy, stupid!" it was this swing 30 percent that was then candidate Bill Clinton's target group. Until 1992, the conservative base was made up of about 65 percent of the electorate. If the Democrats expected to change that percentage, they would have to appeal to that middle group and somehow change their opinion; so that's what Carville set out to do.

On most issues, survey research indicates that the public tends naturally toward the conservative side, with 65 percent conservative opinion and roughly 35 percent on the liberal side. On social issues, the middle 30 percent are generally right of center. This results in the United States electorate being right of center, siding with conservative candidates on most issues. This means that the swing 30 percent has an affinity with the 30 percent on the right. It takes an environment that generates real anxiety before the middle 30 percent will join a coalition of the Left 30 percent. This was the positive environment that Ronald Reagan created and that gave him a solid base of 65 percent of the electorate. And because the swing 30 percent had an affinity with the Right 30 percent, it was convenient for them to walk into Reagan's big tent without an overt fear of being tainted by the other folks who were there.

But here's something else worth noting. The swing 30 has an aversion to the Left. It may not be the most prominent thing in their minds, but they're not feminists or gay activists or extreme environmentalists or doctrinaire labor union supporters. They do not feel comfortable walking into the liberal tent. It takes a lot of fear for their security to override their affinity with the Right and cause them to join a liberal Left coalition. This is why the Left tends to be the movement of fear, advocating big changes and big social adjustments, managed by government to provide security in order to draw people over to their tent.

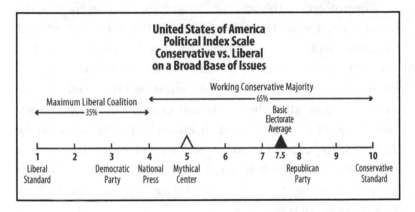

FROM THE OUTSIDE IN

For years, the national media would surmise that middle America, on a 1 to 10 scale, is about a 5, with 1 being most liberal and 10 being most conservative. Therefore, Ronald Reagan and the Republicans, at an 8 or 9 on the media's scale, were out of the mainstream. Since the liberals were just left of 5, around 4 on their scale, they were judged to be closer to the center. But there are two problems within that analysis. First, there is no middle in America, only a 30 percent Right, a 30 percent Left, and a 30 percent swing that leans Right. Second, on a 1 to 10 scale with elected officials like House Speaker Nancy Pelosi at 1 and conservative congressman and presidential candidate Ron Paul at 10—in years past we used Jesse Jackson and Jesse Helms as the benchmarks—the general public comes in at about 7.5. Both Speaker Pelosi and Congressman Paul would be considered on the inside of mainstream politics.

Again, these calculations are based on responses to a wide range of questions covering numerous topics and many years of research. On this scale where a liberal is 1 and a conservative is 10, the Republican Party is an 8, the Democratic Party is a 3, and the national press corps is a 4.

The problem in the past for Democrats was that they had to run as a 3 or 4 to get their party's nomination for president, and then move as quickly as possible toward 7 in the general election. Republican candidates ran for their party's nomination for president as an 8 where they would be fairly well aligned with the public after their National Convention. It was much more difficult for a Democrat to move 4.5 points to the Right than for a Republican to move half a point to the Left for the general election. There was not enough flexibility left in too few issues for the Democratic candidate to make their shift in a short period of time.

It's also important to remember that in good economic times a conservative starts with a broad base of support of around 65 percent of the voting electorate. Because of the affinity/aversion factor, when Democratic candidates try to align the liberal base with the swing 30 percent, they tend to be unsuccessful either in attracting the swing 30 or holding the ideologues in the Left 30 base. This scenario is why very few races on a statewide basis, and certainly the presidential race, have been run under the banner of liberalism.

The liberal base will not sustain a 51 percent majority vote. In fact, the last statewide candidate to run as a true liberal on the principles of liberalism was John Culver in the 1980 U.S. Senate race in Iowa. He lost to Chuck Grassley in that race. Culver received 45.5 percent of the vote while Grassley received 53.5 percent.

The 30 percent Right, as described above, still exists today, as does the 30 percent Left. The swing 30 percent may or may not change their allegiances based upon how the grass roots reconstitutes itself and, as a result of that reorganization, communicates to them. A majority of those in the swing 30 are among the 80 percent followers, especially when it comes to politics. They may be soccer moms or young people concerned about the environment, but they will wait for their options in politics, watching to see which way the momentum is swinging. This is the 30 percent for whom the public opinion wars are generally waged.

The folks in the middle are balanced on a teeter-totter. One end of the teeter-totter represents more government and the promise of security; the other end represents limited government, greater personal freedoms, and the unfettered pursuit of opportunity. The board that runs between them, then, represents public sentiment. As the public becomes more fearful about their economic security, pressure is added to the "more government" side. But as they feel more confident about their economic future, pressure is added to the "less government" side. All things being equal, they're more likely to align with the Right 30 percent. This means the process begins with a little more weight on the "less government" side. And it takes more than an even amount of weight, based on fear or threats of one kind or another, to move the public toward the "more government" side.

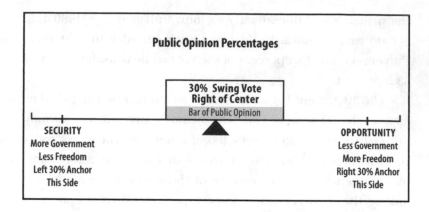

A SOBER WARNING

We don't want government to take over our lives. Unrestricted government authority leads ultimately to total control and restrictions on freedom. Communism and state Socialism, as the best examples of this type of government, always lead to oppression, destruction of the nuclear family, and economic devastation for the nation. We never want to let this nation fall for either of those options, and that's what is really at stake when we take our stand for conservative values at the polls.

We must be vigilant in holding government accountable for how it addresses the prospects of change. The darkness that Ronald Reagan warned us about generally comes disguised as "peace in our time" and "protection for the masses." But no society that has ever fallen for that lie has come through the experienced unscathed. You may be inclined to say, "It could never happen here!" But it will come if we allow it.

The World Economic Forum (WEF) is an organization headquartered in Davos, Switzerland, that advocates the European model for the world's economic system. In the most current meeting held in January 2008, they called for more government management by nation states to moderate the world's impending recession. Further, the United Nations has called for control of the Internet. Its argument is that since the Internet is a worldwide communications and data system and that no one country owns it, then the UN should be charged with regulating and managing it. The UN, along with certain WEF members and the U.S. labor umbrella organization, the AFL-CIO, believe that all labor bargaining in the world should be controlled by the UN in a one-world collective bargaining system. Liberals in the United States have embraced this idea as a "progressive solution." These concepts are presented as a fair way to protect the poor through control of independence. In addition to these ideas, the UN has declared regulation of the world's environment as their domain. By the Kyoto Treaty and other international agreements, the UN desires to manage many aspects of manufacturing and product development in the United States without reference particularly to United States' needs.

If we allow ourselves to become so enamored of the promise of security that we're afraid to turn loose of the security blanket and free ourselves from government subsidies, then we will fall victim to the welfare mentality that leads to darkness and enslavement. If there is ever a major economic shake-up or a long-lasting recession that causes people to run to government for help, the swing 30 will be stuck with the Left 30 for a generation, at which point our freedoms may well disappear.

The message, then, is that we need to be prepared when darkness presents itself. Like every other form of subterfuge, it will come as a compassionate, self-sacrificing service to help the needy and downtrodden. It will speak in warm and caring tones about the plight of single moms with hungry children, the elderly, and the economically deprived. Their proposals then will seem so palatable they're impossible to resist, but no matter how seductive the numbers may appear, they will never equal the cost of your freedom.

If we expect to remain independent and make decisions for ourselves and our families, then we will have to take some responsibility for our own well-being. And, furthermore, we will need to be involved with the well-being of the communities, both religious and secular. Otherwise we may wake up to find ourselves in an inescapable spiritual prison.

Once you've worked your way through the political grid and the societal scale I've provided, you should write out your conclusions on a sheet of paper. I would go so far as to suggest that you prepare a push card (a small handout sheet) with your advice on how to approach the issues of the day, for anyone who may ask for your opinion. You may even want to find some way to post your view on the Internet. You can use the electronic platform provided at www.nuttle.com/momentoftruth. Your personal access code is provided on the inside of the jacket cover of this book. The point is that everyone influences seven to ten people, whether they know it or not. So why not take advantage of this built-in networking possibility? You may be surprised who will follow your lead and ask for your advice.

Mark Sanborn, in his new book, *You Don't Need a Title to Be a Leader,* describes how anyone, anywhere can make a positive difference. It all begins with acting with a purpose and communicating clearly. You'll be surprised how many lives you will impact for each life's good, but also for the collective good of all our lives.[4]

One other result of the 80/20 rule is the way we buy products in this country. If I want to buy a new computer system, I don't do it by becoming an expert in computers. Rather than reading all the consumer reference manuals on rating computer systems and trying to understand how each system works, I will generally ask someone I respect who I know has already done the homework. So they ask me, "What are you looking for, Marc?" And I'll tell them what I have in mind. Then they'll say, "OK. This is how you go about choosing a computer system."

At that point I follow their advice, and most of the time I find that I'm satisfied. Many people in the 80 percent group select political candidates in much the same way. They decide their positions on some of the more complicated issues by asking others what they think. Even if you're in the 80 percent group most of the time, by stating what you believe and explaining your choices to someone else, you may become part of the 20 percent for your peer group.

FOUNDING PRINCIPLES

I never cease to be amazed at the wisdom of our nation's founders. The Declaration of Independence makes the remarkable statement that we are endowed by our Creator with certain unalienable rights; among these are life, liberty, and the pursuit of happiness. The idea that our rights come from the Creator and not from man is anathema to the liberal elites. What this declaration says is that, first, there is a God, and He's real. Second, it says that we have a personal relationship with Him, and, third, we don't have to go to some other organization that controls us to tell us how to be happy. We can do it ourselves by responding to that higher calling.

It took me a long time to understand why the Left cares so intensely about this issue. What difference does it make if I pray in public, pray in school, or acknowledge the authority of God in public and private affairs? Why can't they just leave me alone? But I eventually realized that people will attack, to the death, anything they perceive as a threat to the authority that gives them their rights, their power, and their existence. So if you don't believe in God, what do you believe in? You believe in government. And whether they acknowledge it or not, government is their god. They will perceive anything we do that denies the authority of their god as blasphemy and a crime against mankind.

Therefore they're angry, they're bitter, and they hate you if you don't march to their drummer. If you stand for personal responsibility, individual liberty, and limited government, all of which makes you independent of them and their vision of government as god, then you are automatically the enemy. They don't want to just go do their thing, because without the force of government, nobody will read their propaganda or do what they say. If you go your own way and try to make your own life without them, they will be relegated to irrelevancy. That's why the Left saw Ronald Reagan as a threat, and that's why we have such a deep and bitter division between Left and Right in American society today.

Knowing these things doesn't make the struggle for balance and order any easier. In fact, knowing what motivates the enemy and recognizing the values to which he's committed can increase your workload for a time—which may be why so many people prefer the relative peace of hanging out with the 80 percent. Averting your eyes from danger may make you feel better, but it doesn't mean the danger has gone away.

That's why, throughout these pages, I've kept the focus on the kind of future we want for our children and families, because this is where our noblest and best instincts lie. This was what motivated the freedom-loving men and women of Bulgaria, Ukraine, and Sudan: the knowledge that the sacrifices they make today will help guarantee a better future for their children and their children's children.

You won't need to spend very long scanning the headlines or catching the news on television and radio to grasp the fact that we are at a moment of truth in this country. There are many polarizing forces driving the debates, with candidates on both sides fighting for attention from the media. Every day there's a new poll telling us how the battle is going, who's up and who's down, and, by implication, how we ought to react. The candidates and the media thrive in this environment, but a large majority of the public is at risk of simply tuning out and turning the dial. The 80 percent will say, "I don't have the energy for this. Besides, it'll all come out in the wash." But that's the one option we can't afford to take.

As I pointed out in the first chapters of the book, we're now at the beginning of a new forty-year cycle that will determine what this nation will be and who we will become as a people from this year forward. Many of us may not be around forty years from now, but our children and grandchildren will be here. What sort of world do we want them to inherit? And what are you doing today to make it that way?

MOUTH OF THE DRAGON

Whatever the American people may think of Richard Nixon today, no one can deny that his decision to penetrate the bamboo curtain and force the leaders of that Communist country to enter a dialogue with the free world was one of the most important diplomatic efforts of the twentieth century. I never met him while he was president, but I got to know him very well after he left office. He was friendly and occasionally teased me that he was tired of people asking him how he got my initials, RMN. I knew he had a wonderful memory, but I was flattered that he took the time to think of me and make jokes like that. I hardly ever saw him in this country, but we crossed paths in some of the most unlikely places in the world, such as Ukraine, and he would immediately recognize me and ask what I was up to.

President Nixon loved his country. He was one of the brightest people I've ever known, and he had a strong sense of destiny. He knew that any risk involved in bringing China into the community of nations was more than worth the risk. As a young lawyer, Nixon had read the ominous prediction uttered by Napoleon Bonaparte: "When China awakes, the world will tremble." Later, as a politician, he understood that those words were true. China could not be isolated forever, and Nixon believed it would be much better for the West to have dialogue with the sleeping dragon than to wake up one morning with the dragon at our door.

I tell you this as a point of reference for a congressional hearing I attended as a young lawyer in the early 1980s. I was covering the hearing for a congressional client, in which the committee was interviewing a Chinese dissident seeking political asylum in this country. I was sitting behind the bench and just behind the congressman, facing the witness. I was intrigued by the mannerisms of this middle-aged man. I couldn't help wondering what pressures a man would have to be under to risk his life to escape from Communist China and flee to America seeking political asylum. At the same time, I couldn't help thinking how blessed I was to have been born in this free country.

The witness was nervous and seemed particularly stressed whenever he was asked about his political activities and the persecutions he had endured. He was obviously saddened whenever anyone mentioned his fellow dissidents back in China who were either in hiding, in prison, or missing. But what intrigued me most wasn't the difficulty he had in answering questions about the oppression he endured but answering the most basic questions about his life in China.

When asked where he lived, he explained that he was from a northern province. He had been a ticket puncher at a rural train depot, far away from the town where he had grown up. The congressional panel was curious about how he got to be a ticket puncher: "Who decided that?" he was asked. The man explained that a committee in Beijing processed incoming requests for labor from all across China. The supervisor of that remote train station had requested help, and he was randomly assigned to go to that village and take the job. Regardless of his education, his aptitude, or any occupational skills he might have, he was picked by some faceless, nameless bureaucrat, who knew absolutely nothing about him, and was sent to punch tickets in the North. When he was asked if he had any say in the matter, he was surprised by the question. He said, "No, of course not. You just go where you're told."

What fascinated me was his attitude about the way he had been chosen for the job. There had been many questions that caused him to flinch or show anguish, but the thought of being picked out of a hat and assigned to a remote outpost in the country didn't seem to matter at all. He showed no sign of being upset. The congressmen and their staffs found this very curious. As Americans, they couldn't fathom the idea of being subjected to a process by which your life, your vocation, and your entire future could be decided in such a manner

How could he be so passive about giving up his personal freedom and then respond so intensely, stirred to rebellion by the leaders of the democratic opposition in China when they spoke about the wonders of freedom and individual rights? If those movement leaders had never come to his district, he would still be punching tickets in northern China. Frankly, I don't remember the ultimate outcome in that case. The panel recommended that the petitioner be given provisional asylum and the right to apply for citizenship. But I know for a fact that every man and woman in the room was filled with a profound sense of gratitude for the liberties we, as Americans, enjoy. As the world transitions into a global society, we must be aware of how government control, no matter how well intentioned, can steal from us our independence and freedom.

Today, twenty-five years later, our country faces enormous challenges from the world forces of change, and I have to wonder how we will respond. Will we be passive and compliant like that Chinese dissident as the noose of government control is slipped around our necks, or will we rise up and say, "Beyond this point we will not go!"

This is not an idle question, because the risk of such a dramatic change will be absolutely unavoidable if the majority of voters in this country decides either to stay home on election day and let someone else do it or, worse yet, decides that more and bigger government is the answer to all our problems. When we exercise our right of self-expression in our neighborhoods and in the voting booth, will we be more concerned about our liberty and our children's future, or will we simply bow to the forces of darkness and accept whatever the government decides to give us now for our immediate personal security?

Chapter 11

A RENDEZVOUS WITH DESTINY

You and I have a rendezvous with destiny. We will preserve for our children this, the last best hope of man on Earth, or we will sentence them to take the last step into a thousand years of darkness.[1]
—RONALD REAGAN, 1964

In this final chapter, I would like to summarize my case and appeal to the jury for a fair and reasonable judgment. The case isn't hard to make, but it's not always easy to be heard above the din of clanging symbols and sounding brass in the middle of an election. But this is my appeal: You and I have an obligation to pass on to our children a free and solvent nation. We inherited a solvent government, and we have an obligation to pass on to the next generations as good as we received.

I would add, however, that we should enhance it and add value. Some people may say, "It's not my problem," or "How can I fix something like that?" The answer is simple—you fix it by being part of the solution, by caring about the kinds of leaders you elect, and by holding those in authority accountable for the decisions they make.

As we think about the legacy we will leave to future generations, we need look no further than our obligations as Christians and as citizens of a free nation to stand up against the forces of darkness. The threat of a world managed by experts and bureaucrats is gaining critical mass in many places today. Democratic countries that were once a lighthouse of liberty and democracy to the world are sinking slowly into the darkness of state Socialism and moral decline. Several of the candidates vying for our votes today appear to be totally in sync with the idea of expanding government control and limiting personal freedom. How can we let that pass?

The greatest thing this nation can do for humanity is preserve and protect our liberty, to provide hope for beleaguered peoples everywhere that there is still a place of refuge for those who are oppressed by tyrants promising heaven on earth. Cultures that do not respect individual liberty and freedom from government interference are little more than sitting ducks for the next dictator who happens along. Unfortunately, the problem isn't limited to third-world countries; it's gaining momentum and intensity here too as individuals in government, the universities, and the media continue pushing the European model and calling on Americans to give up our ancient customs and beliefs.

So long as we remain true to the vision of this nation's founders, we will continue to prosper. We may have to stand alone against the world, but that's a challenge we must be willing to take. As Winston Churchill led Great Britain against the forces of evil in Europe during World War II, they literally protected their island and their way of life against all odds at whatever cost. We have good and substantial reasons for protecting what we have. This nation serves as an example to the entire world of what a proper balance between government authority and individual liberty should look like. If that means America is alone against the world, so be it. But, by the same token, we must remain vigilant at home and reject any suggestion from politicians, professors, and pundits that we can sacrifice our freedoms to government control and still remain free.

Since the earliest days of our republic, people have sought these shores for freedom. They came here to escape oppression and injustice in lands that kept them from living their lives as they saw fit. In his book *Mayflower*, Nathaniel Philbrick provides great detail and insight into the personalities, emotions, and motives of the Pilgrims who came here to escape political oppression in the year 1620. He writes about the courage of the Pilgrims crossing deadly seas, and the second wave, the Puritans, who were true believers willing to risk all for their religious convictions.[2] Most of our public schools no longer teach these lessons—too many on the Left now refer to these brave men and women as fanatics and radicals. But nothing could be further from the truth.

From day one, the founders and their descendants and successors have been people of courage and conviction, willing to defend their beliefs with their lives. Maintaining the balance between government's promise of security and the servitude it entails has never been easy. We fought a civil war over it, preferring to survive by our own toil than to accept handouts from the crown heads of Europe.

Despite great sacrifices over the last three hundred years, we have not succumbed to despotism or tyranny. We have remained free. The Constitution, ratified by all thirteen colonies in 1790, was a miracle. For the first time in human history people with diverse interests and cultural backgrounds believed in the concept that in binding themselves together as a nation, all would be protected. The eloquence of the Federalist Papers on this matter introduced a new philosophy of government to the world. And that philosophy has served us well.

FREEDOM OR SERVITUDE

In the 1830s, Alexis de Tocqueville traveled throughout the United States to research the beliefs and practices of the people of this new nation. He chronicled his findings in his two-volume book *Democracy in America*. During his journeys, he set out to compare America's executive, legislative, and judicial procedures to those of France and other European countries, and he asked many penetrating questions about what the future of democracy would yield. He questioned whether or not people would be willing to give up all they had in exchange for what government would promise. He writes:

> Our contemporaries are constantly excited by two conflicting passions: they want to be led, and they wish to remain free. As they cannot destroy either the one or the other of these contrary propensities, they strive to satisfy them both at once. They devise a sole, tutelary, and all-powerful form of government, but elected by the people. They combine the principles of centralization and that of popular sovereignty; this gives them a respite: they console themselves for being in tutelage by the reflection that they have chosen their own guardians. Every man allows himself to be put in leading-strings because he sees that it is not a person or a class of persons, but the people at large who hold the end of his chain.
>
> By this system, the people shake off their state of dependence just long enough to select their master and then relapse into it again. A great many persons at the present day are quite contented with this sort of compromise between administrative despotism and the sovereignty of the people; and they think they have done enough for the protection of individual freedom when they have surrendered it to the power of the nation at large. This does not

satisfy me: the nature of him I am to obey signifies less to
me than the fact of extorted obedience.[3]

The nature of the French statesman's concern is apparent:
Will the Americans be able to avoid the yoke of despotism by
not becoming a slave to the government from which they desire
to be independent? Or will they sacrifice their independence
for the security of the all-powerful state? Today, more than 175
years after de Tocqueville posed the question, we must answer
the question. Will we remain vigilant in our relationship to
government, or will we compromise and, in so doing, toss our
children's future to the wind?

When my forefathers came to Oklahoma in the last century,
they expected exactly what President Sarkozy related in his
speech to the American people in 2007. No one told them, "Come
and everything will be given to you." They merely said "Come
and make a life for yourself by your own talent and courage."
The Oklahoma settlers came for the promise of a homestead,
but nothing else from the government was expected. They were
true pioneers, much like the Pilgrims in their quest for freedom
and self-determination. They trusted that their destiny was a
relationship with their God and their family, and they had an
obligation to protect it.

Have you ever wondered what questions your children will
ask you twenty-five years from now about the state of freedom
in your day? Will they have the opportunities you had? Will the
government be their facilitator or their master by that time? In
1984, twenty years into the last forty-year cycle of this nation's
political history, Ronald Reagan was at his zenith. He won forty-
nine of fifty states in that election. The nation believed in and
followed his leadership.

Twenty years from now, we can still be the greatest nation
on the earth and the last best hope of man on the earth, or we
can go the other way. Will we remain a beacon of freedom to the

world? Will you lead those who depend on you? Or will we have taken those fatal first steps into a thousand years of darkness. If the tone of your children's question is, "What happened? Why don't I have the same opportunities you had?" what will you say to them? As Reagan admonished us, let us at least be able to say, "I saw it coming. I didn't hide. I did all I could."

My children today pursue independent careers. One is a small-business owner; one is in ministry. They deal with government and they know that government has a place in an ordered society. But they seek their direction and their daily purpose from the One who created them. And they understand that their freedom to do so is a matter of right. I want my own legacy to my children to be that I did everything in my power to protect that right for them and their families. And my prayer each day is that, together, we will pass the torch of liberty to America's children, from generation to generation, for as long as this nation shall endure.

THINKING ABOUT TOMORROW

If you're anxious about the future and you fear that you're not going to be able to pass on to your children a society as good as the one you had, you're going to be in turmoil. But there are other things on the horizon that will make the situation even more intense—terrorism, the rise of China, the Internet, nonstate states, and all the things I've described in the previous chapter. These are all complicating factors. We see it, but what are we going to do? The answer is, we have to take action.

Think about what you would do in the face of a serious challenge. First, you have to define yourself and your most important concerns. Then you define how you address government in line with your spiritual values. Then you prioritize your issues pursuant to the grid I presented in chapter 3—or something similar of your own design—and finalize your grid. Then you have to take some leadership. Everybody has ten people who look to them for information—it may be your spouse, your kids, the people you work with, your friends, the people in your church, or the guy next door, but we all have people who want to know what we think about the issues. They're already looking for you.

Once you have defined yourself and your values, then you know what your limits are. These are your backstop. There is in most critical issues a point beyond which you will not yield. Now what do you want to give your children? What do you want them to have in twenty-five years? This means you have to define your freedom. In China people can't move around freely. They can't travel without papers. We say we will never allow that to happen here, but are we so sure of that? What if there were another terrorist attack on the American heartland? What if some other tragedy were to change the landscape? You can think about the unthinkable, and you can educate your kids. But you will need to define your values and set a path for maintaining them.

Currently, the field running for president has narrowed dramatically. How do you evaluate your options? First, of course, you know that you're not going to evade the questions; you're going to dig in and find out what you need to know. Second, you're going to trust yourself to make a reasonable judgment based on your commitment to freedom and limited government. You will say to yourself, "Here's who I am, and here's what I believe. Here's what I want for my family." Trust in your convictions, and be at peace.

Do you understand the definition of a spiritual prison? An example of a spiritual prison would be the four mayors I met in Bulgaria, who worried that they might have to stay in a Communist state because they wanted to keep the government's ration of hay and milk. For the promise of hay and milk they would have refused to join the freedom movement or to vote for the constitution of a new democratic republic. For hay and milk they could easily have thrown away the blessings of liberty. But was such a paltry bribe really worth the risk?

How about more familiar circumstances? One spiritual prison may be your job and what you're locked into. Another may be that you're confused because of something in which you're involved. Some people might be in a spiritual prison because of their addictions to personal pleasure and the moral looseness of contemporary society. What is it that's keeping you from enjoying the blessings of liberty and the freedom to make your own choices? Personal habits and fears can become prisons as well, but thinking about these issues may help you sort through the various complications and commitments in your life and decide if you may be in a spiritual prison.

HOW YOU DEFINE FREEDOM

A part of my purpose in reviewing these things is to help me define the future I want for my children. The Pilgrims, the Puritans, the Cavaliers of Virginia, and all those brave souls who came here so long ago had to make similar decisions. What did the people of that era want for the future? And what did they desire for the future of their children? The answer in that case is not difficult: it was freedom, and it happened to be religious freedom most of all.

They made great sacrifices of their own comfort and safety to find a place in the world where they could worship God and live in a reasonable balance with government. Most had left behind their comfortable lives in Europe, bringing children and their pregnant wives in small boats across an angry sea in the dead of winter. They didn't ask for government support. They just said, "Leave us alone." That's one way to define freedom. But you will have to define it for yourself and your children's future.

Now concerning the issues of our day—immigration, energy independence, taxation, jobs, the environment—the process is much the same. You determine your priorities. Admittedly, these are complicated issues, and you're going to have to do some homework to find out what you like and don't like. But that's called democracy, and it's a participatory process. But, further, if you're a small-business owner, you know you really have to pay attention to such things.

This is something I've had the opportunity to tell some of the Republican presidential candidates in the 2008 race. Small business is a vital part of our economy, and small-business owners are one of the largest conservative constituencies in the nation. Fully 50 percent of the non–farm adult workforce in this country is either owned by or works for small business. Survey after survey shows that the American people like small-business owners. Nobody dislikes them. Nobody distrusts them. Nobody thinks they're the root of the problem.

To stand up and say that small business is an important and valuable part of the community would seem to be the most natural thing a political candidate could do these days. The American people are unique in our love for freedom, and there are no better defenders of essential American values than the men and women in small business today. These are the people who support the small towns, the high school band, the sports programs, and the kids. Any candidate who tells the nation that he or she will do everything in their power to maintain the ability of small-business owners to prosper and help bring the country into the twenty-first century by creating jobs and opportunities will be hitting a home run.

I've made the point that if I'm right and forces are coming that are going to make us choose between our traditional commitment to individual liberty and the European model of state Socialism, then we need to know who will be standing beside us. Are we going to be standing alone? The world will challenge us in the next decade in ways we can't begin to imagine. I think we know that this will happen, even if we have no way of knowing when and where those challenges will come.

But we don't need to fear tomorrow. Jesus said, in the familiar King James rendering, "Take therefore no thought for the morrow: for the morrow shall take thought for the things of itself. Sufficient unto the day is the evil thereof" (Matt. 6:34, KJV). We simply need to trust God and be prepared to stand on principle. But we also need to stand, as Reagan said in his speech, as the last great hope of man on the earth. America is the only nation in the world where we have the freedom to do whatever we wish with our families for their benefit—through education, through the jobs we choose, and through the freedom to practice our faith as we see fit. Let us never relinquish that freedom or merely let it slip away unnoticed. Think of others worldwide. What would happen to hope if the United States were lost as an island of freedom? Where in the world would the Pilgrims have escaped? We have an obligation to the world to protect the safe harbor of our island of freedom.

WHO ARE YOU, REALLY?

Are you the 80 percenter or the 20 percenter? Where do you see yourself in the 30/30/30 mix? What's important is not where you fit but knowing that you do fit and then deciding how you will use your talents and skills to make a difference. There's nothing wrong with the way you're designed: the Lord wired us all in different ways. Having said that, I hope you understand the threat of too large a government. But there will naturally be a range of opinion, and that's where you begin.

You can be a swing voter and not be on the hard-Right or the hard-Left. But if you're in the 20 percent category, then you have a responsibility to engage the issues on a personal level, to be informed on the subjects that really matter, and to use your influence to help bring about positive results. If you do any less than that, I would have to say you're probably not living up to your full potential. You're not going out and activating; you're just putting in your time.

If you're part of the 80 percent, you're most likely a follower. You're doing your duty by keeping your eyes open and responding to your natural inclinations and choices, and that's fine. But don't let yourself be drawn in by the smiles and sweet talk of some of our candidates about all the good things the government can do for you—so you won't have to do things for yourself. You might be surprised how many people will buy a political candidate the same way they buy a TV, a stereo, or a sofa. The more appealing the pretty pictures and the more comforting the sales pitch, the easier they part with their cash and buy the goods. But what have they really got? And will they be satisfied when they find out what they've got? Ask, what has a government-provided benefit cost me in terms of loss of freedom?

Before buying a pretty sales pitch, stop and think about what's really at stake. What are you getting, and what are you being promised in return? What do you think? At the very least, you need to read about the candidates, listen to what they say, and talk to people you trust about the issues and the choices you're being asked to make, and then make your own decision.

You can, of course, make a decision not to make a decision. I can find no requirement in the New Testament that says you have to make a decision to be political, and I find nothing that says you shouldn't. But the American democracy is built on the premise that you, as a free and independent citizen, have a duty to help select the leaders of the nation and the community. To do that, you need to look at the issues carefully before you make your choice. We're on an island in a sea of hidden agendas. Storms are coming, and we need to make decisions about how we're going to deal with the situation in Washington. And I can't imagine how the storms in this tempestuous political sea won't sink you if you merely choose to do nothing at all.

From the beginning of this work, I've tried to make the point that every American has to think about what they have in life and what they're obligated to give back. Will you leave the world a better place when you go? Will you be able to tell your children and grandchildren that you did all you could do? I mean, who are you really? If you've made it to this point in the book, I'm sure you'll have many reactions, and I hope you agree with me about the importance of the freedoms you enjoy and the risks we will face if we allow others to determine the future for us. So let me briefly recap where we've been. Over the last ten chapters, I've laid out my case in these seven areas:

1. A government that becomes too big and provides too many services that we should provide for ourselves is a *threat* to our freedom and can enslave us in a spiritual prison. All government programs should be evaluated for their impact on loss of individual freedom and the threat to our children's future.

2. The world is in great transition caused by world forces outside our control.

3. The United States finds itself at the end of a forty-year cycle that will require us to make key decisions about our future course as a country.

4. Because of this world pressure and change, people feel anxious and uneasy about their

destiny and are looking for hope and new leadership.

5. The United States is unique in its culture of economic, religious, and personal freedom, and, as an island of these freedoms, we are at risk of becoming compromised with the rest of the world.

6. As citizens of this great nation, we have an obligation to take a stand and lead others in finding the way.

7. We are not alone in this world in our desire for freedom and a better future for our children. Therefore we have a moral imperative to do everything we can to protect our island of freedom for all future generations of the world.

This is what I call my elevator speech. I do it with political candidates whenever I ask them why they're running for office. Sometimes they give me a half dozen vague reasons, and I have to tell them they have to be able to explain what they hope to accomplish in a ten-second sound bite. Any longer and they've lost the audience.

12 STEPS FOR THE MORAL IMPERATIVE	
Knowledge:	1. The country is in great anxiety—America's future is under attack.
	2. Friends and family believe you and want your leadership.
	3. World pressures are mounting and will challenge our immediate future.
	4. America has a critical role to play in survival of world freedom.

12 STEPS FOR THE MORAL IMPERATIVE	
Solutions:	5. An individual must take responsibility for their own future. This involves duty, obligation, and sacrifice.
	6. Small business and family-owned business are keys to growth in the American economy.
	7. Think in generational terms (three—past, present, and future)
	8. Support limited government and understand the security versus freedom balance and ratio.
Action:	9. Define yourself and your values.
	10. Prioritize your issues.
	11. Communicate your values—lead others in your sphere of influence—illustrate your confidence.
	12. Trust in your faith.

Maybe that's something you'd like to consider. Can you define who you are and what you want to accomplish in a ten-second sound bite? It's worth a try. My purpose in writing this book was first to seek God's purpose fulfilled in each of us as He designed. I would love to give my readers the comfort and peace of knowing that we have a living hope for all eternity and a God-given purpose in this life as well. And part of our purpose is to help shape the world we live in for succeeding generations.

APPLYING WHAT YOU BELIEVE

We have the privilege of living in communities where our voice and our vote can make a difference. Many of us have children, relatives, and friends who listen to us and who care about the things that concern us. And, politically, we have the right and privilege of sharing our beliefs and our hopes with others. That's one of the fundamental rights granted by the First Amendment and a cornerstone of the American democratic system.

But, practically, how do you do that? How can you provide peace, comfort, and security for your family, and project that to others who need to hear your views? We all need to know what to do, and we need the input of those who have considered the issues from a position of wisdom. As I've considered the implications of the 80/20 rule, I've come to the conclusion that I'm part of the 20 percent, and I'm supposed to lead and be active. When people come to me and say, "Marc, I'm worried. Between illegal immigration, al Qaeda, recession, and the rising cost of gasoline, I'm really uncertain about what the future may hold for me and my family. What do you think? What are you doing about all that?" I want to have an answer.

To be ready for that question, I go back to my grid. I make my decisions about what I believe in each of those critical areas, and I don't hesitate to say what I believe. In a political season like this one, I want to be prepared to tell at least ten people what I've discovered to help them consider the issues and the implications of their vote. I make a personal commitment to be active, to remember what's at stake, and to remain confident and move forward with my life.

Polls and surveys in recent months tell us that the economy has now surpassed immigration as one of the hottest issues in the upcoming elections. The economy will be an issue throughout the 2008 election cycle. There are folks with a more global outlook who seem to feel that retaining our American identity and customs is old-fashioned and xenophobic. We need to open the gates and make way for change. But, you know what? It's OK to be an American. There's nothing wrong with the American economic model, and our customs are honorable and good. The way we've been doing things for the last two hundred twenty years is an example to the world, and it's still working. There's nothing wrong with this country. It's OK to be an American.

One of the things I mean by that is that when immigrants of any kind come to this country, they need to abide by certain obligations. There are responsibilities involved in being an American, and first among these is the requirement to speak the language, English. Number two, they have to pay taxes like everyone else. If they don't like the taxes we're asked to pay, then they can participate in government through the political process and have a say at the polls like everyone else.

Too often the forces of political correctness get the balance wrong. It's true, we must be sensitive to other people's needs, but only as it benefits the whole of society. If you have trouble thinking about this on a national scale, think about it in terms of your church. When you go to church, does everybody speak a separate language? Do you just worry about your own needs or the needs of your small group? Do you demand that the sermon be what you want to hear, regardless how it speaks to everyone else in the church? Or do you work together as individual members of the body of Christ, actively seeking out ways to serve others and grow in the faith?

Which of those two models would be the kind of church that Paul described in his letters? In his second letter to Timothy, the apostle says we are to "avoid foolish and ignorant disputes, knowing that they generate strife." And he adds that "a servant of the Lord must not quarrel but be gentle to all, able to teach, patient, in humility correcting those who are in opposition…" (2 Tim. 2:23–25). A spirit of cooperation and participation is essential, and that lesson applies as well to citizenship as it does to the Christian life.

Christians are to respect one another and even to love one another. If that's good enough for the church, why isn't it good enough for the country? When people come here from third-world countries, do they stop to ask themselves, "Now, what is my obligation to the United States?" If they become a citizen, they have to take an oath of loyalty, but who talks to them about other things? Someone needs to say, "Welcome to America. But here are some basic rules: You have to obey the laws and get an education, and here's how that works. You have to speak English, and you have to assimilate, and here's how you do it."

That doesn't mean they have to give up their own history or culture, but when immigrants settle here, they become Americans, and that means they're bound by our laws to support the values and practices of this constitutional republic. If they can't accept that, then maybe they don't belong here at all.

Some people, including some politicians, would say, "Well, if you got here illegally and you're working now, who am I to throw you out?" But what does that say about the importance of our laws and customs? If you can break that law with impunity, what other laws can you break? Where does it end? That's a one-way ticket to a lawless society and the end of American culture as we know it.

NEVER GIVE IN!

As I've listed the issues of concern in this election year, from energy to immigration, my objective has been to make a case for citizen involvement in the political process and to encourage every American to take the health and well-being of this great nation as their personal responsibility. If you and I do not look to these matters every day and take seriously the claims and the threats of those who would diminish our freedom, we will have only ourselves to blame when this wonderful way of life is gone.

Freedom is not free. Those words have never been truer than now. When Thomas Jefferson said, "The price of freedom is eternal vigilance,"[4] he wasn't talking about King George or the redcoats; he was talking about those people in our midst who would, by expanding the size and reach of government, subtly rob us of our legacy and subject us to involuntary servitude.

The issues I've addressed in these pages have been those I thought were of immediate importance. Among them are issues such as taxation, Social Security, Medicaid, and Medicare. If you haven't been paying attention, maybe you didn't know that government's security network is overextended. The entire system will soon be broken. But who will fix it? We have no long-term planning, and the political parties spend their time jockeying for applause, seeing who can amuse the largest number with witty sound bites. It is moral negligence for my generation to say, "I'm going to make it until I die, and I don't care if the country is bankrupt when I'm gone." But the fact that there is no twenty-five-year plan in place to fix this broken system is, in my opinion, criminal negligence.

If you want to participate in government, you can. And if you feel the desire to be part of a movement, or to start one, then I hope you will do that. Talking about it isn't enough. Wishful thinking isn't enough. It will take imagination and personal sacrifice to come up with a system that will benefit future generations. The founders didn't think twice about making those sacrifices, but when Alexis de Tocqueville came here, he asked the question: will the American people be willing to make the sacrifices necessary for the people to provide for their own needs, or will they buy the politician's argument, "I'll give you everything for free"?

The saying is true: "There's no such thing as a free lunch." Everything comes with a price, but the question is, what price are you willing to pay? The price of hard work and planning for the future, the price of putting restraints on the appetites of the liberal tax-and-spend cartel in Washington, or the price of government involvement and control in every area of your life?

I've written repeatedly in these pages about Ronald Reagan's remarks in 1964, which awakened the conservative movement. In light of all these issues, I would like to mention one of the most stirring speeches in the annals of freedom, delivered by Winston Churchill at Harrow School in October 1941, when the British people were suffering under daily bombardments from Nazi warplanes. Here is the entire text of those remarks:

> This is the lesson: never give in, never give in, never, never, never, never—in nothing, great or small, large or petty— never give in except to convictions of honour and good sense. Never yield to force; never yield to the apparently overwhelming might of the enemy.[5]

Sometimes the enemy is armed with bombs and rockets, but sometimes he comes with smiles and banners and red, white, and blue bunting. Sometimes, he comes with a remote control, an easy chair, and a cold drink and says, "Don't worry about it! What can one person really do?" He may come with any of a hundred excuses to take your eye off the objective. But if there's one thing the patriots of 1776 wanted us to remember, it's that we're responsible for what happens next. It's about the type of government you want now and in the future. What can you do now that will make life better for your family and your nation? What can you do to hold back the darkness?

This is what you must decide. Do you volunteer? Do you become more active in politics? Do you participate in group discussions? Do you write a column or a blog on the Internet? Do you run for elective office yourself or give your support to someone who truly understands what needs to be done? What are you going to do? There are a million ways you can make a difference, but the one thing you must not do is sit back and say, "It's not my fault, and I'm going to let somebody else worry about it."

Unlike the brave men and women I met in Eastern Europe and East Africa, people in this country don't tend to think generationally. People in my own generation haven't been forced to consider very many "What if?" scenarios; we haven't been hit over the head with a two-by-four and forced to think about what may happen if we fail to exercise due diligence. If they ever come to that point, I think they'll be responsible. But will it be soon enough?

THIRD WAVE OF LEADERSHIP

These are transitional times. How we respond to them will ultimately result in one of two possible futures. America will either stand alone as an island of freedom in a sea of foreign bureaucracies, or we will bow to the yoke of Europeanization and life in our private spiritual prisons. The path we choose will depend on what we decide in the coming year and the leadership we empower in the elections of 2008. Will we turn back the clock and follow the path of servitude to big government, or will we make a new commitment to personal liberty and limited government? If we choose the latter path, as I hope we will, we're going to need leaders who understand our passion and will pledge to make our battles their own. I call such men and women the third wave of leadership.

The first wave was led by Ronald Reagan. The second was led by bold men and women at the state and national levels who followed in his footsteps. This second wave included all the leaders who emerged in 1975 on the Christian Right, the New Right, and the supply-side Right. Jerry Falwell, James Dobson, and Pat Robertson led the Christian Right to a national movement. Newt Gingrich, with "The Contract for America" in 1994, captured control of Congress for the Republicans. And President George W. Bush maintained the Reagan coalition through the 2000 and 2004 election cycles.

The third wave will gain full force as the collective actions of individuals, one by one, change the cultural dynamic by taking responsibility for the future of this nation, using their talents, resources, and deepest passions to preserve our great cultural heritage. This third wave of leadership is not only critical to pursuing a new birth of freedom, but it is also absolutely essential to our survival as a free people.

Clark Mitchell is the young pastor of a dynamic evangelical church called Journey Church, where I am a member. The church has realized phenomenal growth by committing itself to the belief that God can do anything if you just believe in His sovereignty and power. The church's goal is to transform a city, one person at a time, and have a blast in the process. Clark is a leader of the third wave category. In the Old Testament, God raised up prophets to lead Israel. In the New Testament, God raised up leaders to build the church. Now, in the third wave, churches are being raised up to transform communities. Leaders such as Clark Mitchell are finding innovative and creative ways to solve the problems of society without giving up personal freedom.

As you define yourself, your beliefs, and your priorities, please remember that there's a fundamental philosophical difference between what we believe as Americans and what so many people in other nations believe. Our forefathers wrote eloquently about the duties of free men and the sovereignty of God in a democratic republic. They believed that in a democracy, God is sovereign over both man and government, and man is sovereign over government. Modern liberalism, on the other hand, believes government is God and sovereign over man. Dictatorships and monarchies believe a man can be both God and government, and is sovereign over man. To take the comparison one step further, I would add that followers of Islam believe that God is government and sovereign over man. America is the only nation founded on the basic principle that a person is sovereign over government.

I can't think of what our forefathers sacrificed for our freedoms without feeling a deep sense of gratitude and pride. But there are times when I can't help wondering if we've lost our appreciation for what we have inherited. It's time to look at our lives in generational terms—perhaps this is something the Chinese can teach us. We've inherited such a great country from our fathers and mothers. They helped advance the American Dream and protected us all from assault in World War II. The current generation has made some important strides, but we're consuming more than we've produced. It's unfair to take from the next generation that which is necessary for our own pleasure and convenience in the present. But that's what we are doing if we don't make some adjustments in our thinking and our policies. Regardless of the 2008 election results, our commitment continues. We must determine our point of balance between government-provided security and our self-determined freedom to pursue opportunity. Each of us must face spiritually our own *moment of truth*.

We have a moral imperative to at least give the next generation the same footing, the same foundation, the same freedoms, and the same hope that we received from the previous generation. I would urge you at a time such as this to step out of your comfort zone, to take up a cause greater than yourself, and to pursue it with passion and make a contribution to this new third wave of leadership.

We have a responsibility to never take even one step toward a thousand years of darkness. Darkness is too much government taking too much freedom for too little in return. It's much better to defend the balance we've been guaranteed by the Constitution with every breath we take, regardless of the cost. We must never give in to the temptation to let someone else do for us what only we can do for ourselves. Our children are too precious and their future too critical to the legacy of generations for us to be any less so resolved.

Notes

PREFACE—THE CRUCIBLE OF CHANGE

1. Ronald W. Reagan, "A Time for Choosing" (a speech in support of the candidacy of Barry Goldwater, Republican National Convention, San Francisco, California, October 27, 1964). Transcript available at http://www.reaganfoundation.org/reagan/speeches/rendezvous.asp (accessed January 17, 2008).
2. Ibid.
3. Ibid.

CHAPTER 1—FOR SUCH A TIME AS THIS

1. *Julius Caesar*, 4.3. Reference provided by Massachusetts Institute of Technology, *The Complete Works of William Shapespeare*, http://shakespeare.mit.edu/julius_caesar/julius_caesar.4.3.html (accessed February 1, 2008). References are to act and scene.
2. John Whitesides, "Americans Enter Holidays in Dark Mood: Poll," Reuters, November 21, 2007, http://www.reuters.com/article/newsOne/idUSL2165210520071121 (accessed November 30, 2007). See the full Reuters/Zogby Index in chart form at: http://www.reuters.com/news/globalcoverage/rzi.
3. Gary Langer, "Poll: A Year Before '08 Election, Public's Theme Is Discontent," ABC News Polling Unit, November 4, 2007, http://abcnews.go.com/PollingUnit/story?id=3813959&page=1 (accessed November 21, 2007).
4. The Declaration of Independence, http://www.ushistory.org/declaration/document/ (accessed January 17, 2008).
5. Ronald W. Reagan, "A Time for Choosing." *Editor's Note:* There are at least two versions of Mr. Reagan's remarks at the 1964 Republican Convention in circulation—a version of the speech as originally written, and the version that was actually presented on the live television broadcast from San Francisco. This discussion incorporates some elements of each.
6. Congressional Record: Daily Digest, January 20, 1995, D63–D68.
7. BrainyQuote, "Plutarch Quotes," http://www.brainyquote.com/quotes/authors/p/plutarch.html (accessed January 17, 2008).
8. Howard K. Smith, as quoted by Charles McVey, *Our American Times*, "The Danger of Government: Part 1, President Reagan's Convention Speech," September 20, 2005, http://209.85.207.104/search?q=cache:KI7EhTU8ib0J:www.ouramericantimes.com/assets/pdfs/OATs_Part1_Reagan_050922.pdf+The+profit+motive+is+outmoded.+It+must+be+replaced+by+the+incentives+of+the+welfare+state&hl=en&ct=clnk&cd=4&gl=us (accessed January 17, 2008).

9. Ronald Reagan, *An American Life* (New York: Simon and Schuster, 1990), 213. A version of the text is available at http://www .ronaldreagan.com/primaries.html (accessed January 17, 2008).

10. Benjamin Franklin, Pennsylvania Assembly: Reply to the Governor, November 11, 1755.

11. Milton Friedman with Rose D. Friedman, *Capitalism and Freedom* (Chicago: University of Chicago Press, 1982), preface.

CHAPTER 2—MILESTONES ON THE JOURNEY

1. University of Virginia, "Thomas Jefferson on Politics and Government: 34. Public Works & Public Assistance," http://etext.lib.virginia .edu/jefferson/quotations/jeff1310.html (accessed February 4, 2008).

2. Amity Shlaes, *The Forgotten Man: A New History of the Great Depression* (New York: HarperCollins, 2007).

3. James T. Patterson, *The American Presidency* (Scholastic Library Resources), s.v. "The New Deal," http://ap.grolier.com/ article?assetid=0285400-00&templatename=/article/article.html (accessed January 18, 2008).

4. Samuel Rutherford, *Lex, Rex, or the Law and the Prince* (Harrisonburg, VA: Sprinkle Publications, 1982).

5. Quote DB, "John Adams Quotes," http://www.quotedb.com/ quotes/3659 (accessed January 18, 2008).

6. Thinkexist.com, "John Adams Quotes," http://thinkexist.com/ quotation/our_constitution_was_made_only_for_a_moral_and/262425 .html (accessed January 18, 2008).

7. Exit-poll results and a fascinating survey of the differences in values between Democrats and Republicans in the presidential election of 2004 are available at BeliefNet.org online at: http://www.beliefnet.com/ story/155/story_15546.html.

CHAPTER 3—RELIGIOUS TOLERANCE IN REVERSE

1. The White House, "President Bush Signs Partial Birth Abortion Ban Act of 2003," http://www.whitehouse.gov/news/releases/2003/11/20031105-1 .html (accessed January 18, 2008).

2. For a summary of Gov. Romney's remarks, see: Lisa Riley Roche, "Romney's Speech Champions 'Symphony of Faith,'" Deseret Morning News, Dec. 7, 2007, http://deseretnews.com/dn/view/0,5143,695233936,00.html (accessed December 17, 2007).

3. The Declaration of Independence, "Declaration Text," http://www .ushistory.org/declaration/document/index.htm (accessed January 19, 2008).

4. Jonathan Darman, "Mitt Romney 2008: America's First Mormon President? The New England Republican Who Might Make It So" *Newsweek*, December 25, 2006, http://www.mittromney.com/News/In-The-News/ Mitt_Romney_2008x_Americaxs_First_Mormon_Presidentx_The_New_ England_Republican_Who_Might_Make_It_So (accessed January 19, 2008).

5. Newt Gingrich, *Real Change: From the World That Fails to the World That Works* (Washington DC: Regnery, 2008).

6. Michael Luo, "Romney Seeks to Defuse Concerns Over Mormon Faith," *New York Times*, December 7, 2007, http://www.nytimes.com/2007/12/07/us/politics/06cnd-romney.html?pagewanted=print (accessed January 19, 2008).

7. Benjamin Franklin, Speech to the Constitutional Convention, June 28, 1787. Manuscript notes by Franklin are preserved in the Library of Congress.

8. United States Constitutional Convention, Max Farrand, *The Records of the Federal Convention of 1787* (New Haven, CT: Yale University Press, 1911), 471.

9. ConstitutionFacts.com, "Famous Quotes," http://www.constitutionfacts.com/index.cfm?section=funZone&page=famousQuotes.cfm (accessed January 19, 2008).

CHAPTER 4—THE QUALITIES OF A LEADER

1. Russell Kirk, "Ten Conservative Principles," The Russell Kirk Center for Cultural Renewal, http://www.kirkcenter.org/kirk/ten-principles.html (accessed January 19, 2008).

2. Pat Robertson, *Courting Disaster: How the Supreme Court Is Usurping the Power of the Congress and the People* (Nashville, TN: Integrity Publishers, 2004), 159–160.

3. Mark Gerzon, *A House Divided* (New York: Jeremy Tarcher, 1996).

4. David Boren, *A Letter to America* (Norman, OK: University of Oklahoma Press, 2008).

CHAPTER 5—FOR THE COMMON GOOD

1. Joyce Appleby and Terrance Ball, eds., *Jefferson: Political Writings* (New York: Cambridge University, 1999), 244.

2. Alexis de Tocqueville, George Lawrence, trans., J. P. Mayer, ed., *Democracy in America*, vol. 2 (New York: Harper & Row, 1988), 133.

3. Ibid., 526.

4. Ibid., 529.

5. Ted Baker, *Doing Well by Doing Good: The Bottom Line on Workplace Practices* (Washington DC: Economic Policy Institute, 1999).

6. Adam Smith, *The Wealth of Nations* (New York: Bantam Classics, 2003), 184.

7. Ibid.

8. The Avalon Project at Yale Law School, "The Federalist Papers: No. 51," http://www.yale.edu/lawweb/avalon/federal/fed51.htm (accessed January 19, 2008).

9. Ibid.

10. Bartleby.com, "John Bartlett (1820–1905) Familiar Quotations, 10 ed., 1990," http://www.bartleby.com/100/777.24.html (accessed January 19, 2008).

CHAPTER 6—A BASE DIVIDED

1. As quoted by Robert P. George in *Making Men Moral: Civil Liberties and Public Morality* (New York: Oxford University Press, USA, 1995), 63.

2. Jim Wallis is president of the liberal activist organization Sojourners; Richard Cizik is vice president for governmental affairs of the National Association of Evangelicals and an advocate of climate-change reforms; Rick Warren, senior pastor of Saddleback Church in Southern California, has used profits from his best-selling book, *The Purpose-Driven Life*, to fund AIDS activism in Africa and to draw attention to global warming and environmental issues.

3. Jim Wallis, *The Great Awakening: Reviving Faith and Politics in a Post–Religious Right America* (New York: HarperOne, 2008).

4. Patrick Buchanan, *Day of Reckoning: How Hubris, Ideology, and Greed Are Tearing America Apart* (New York: St. Martin's Press, 2007).

5. F. A. Hayek, ed. Bruce Caldwell, *The Road to Serfdom* (Chicago, IL: University of Chicago Press, 2007).

6. David Aikman, "A Report on Christianity in China: A Conversation With David Aikman," Speech at the Ethics and Public Policy Center in Washington, September 26, 2002.

7. Idem., *Jesus in Beijing: How Christianity Is Changing the Global Balance of Power* (Washington DC: Regnery, 2003), 5.

8. Barry Aarons et al., "France Gets It Right; Can U.S. Politicians Do the Same?" IPI PolicyBytes, November 13, 2007, http://www .policybytes.org/blog/policybytes.nsf/dx/taxbytes-4.43-france-gets -it-right-can-u.s.-politicians-do-the-same.htm (accessed January 19, 2008).

CHAPTER 7—THE CHALLENGE OF GLOBALISM

1. ThinkExist.com, "Winston Churchill Quotes," http://thinkexist .com/quotation/kites_rise_highest_against_the_wind-not_with_it/9540. html (accessed February 11, 2008).

2. Laura Donnelly and Patrick Sawer, "Record Numbers Go Abroad for Health," *London Sunday Telegraph*, October 28, 2007, http://www.telegraph .co.uk/global/main.jhtml?xml=/global/2007/10/28/noindex/nhealth128.xml (accessed December 28, 2007).

CHAPTER 8—WHERE LIBERTY IS DENIED

1. QuoteDB.com, "Thomas Jefferson Quotes," http://www .quotedb.com/quotes/2530 (accessed January 19, 2008).

2. Jesse Green, "Can Disney Build a Better Mickey Mouse?" *New York Times*, April 18, 2004, http://www.nytimes.com/2004/04/18/movies/ 18GREE.html?pagewanted=1&ei=5007&en=53509b9f98996f41&ex= 1397620800&partner=USERLAND (accessed January 19, 2008).

3. The Quotations Page, "Classic Quotes: Thomas Hobbes," http:// www.quotationspage.com/quote/34608.html (accessed January 20, 2008).

4. Infoplease.com, Encyclopedia, "Yeltsin, Boris Nikolayevich," http://www.infoplease.com/ce6/people/A0853041.html (accessed January 20, 2008).

5. Ibid.

CHAPTER 9—OUT OF THE DARKNESS

1. BrainyQuote.com, "Learned Hand Quotes," http://www.brainyquote.com/quotes/authors/l/learned_hand.html (accessed January 20, 2008).

2. Milton Friedman and Rose D. Friedman, "The Tide in the Affairs of Men," *The Freeman*, April 1989. (An abridged version of this essay is available at http://www.fee.org/publications/notes/notes/theTide.asp (accessed January 20, 2008).

CHAPTER 10—WORLD FORCES OF CHANGE

1. Inspirational Public Art, Dialogue Project, "Spiritual Quotes," http://www.dialogueproject.net/dialogue/subject/fspirit.html (accessed January 20, 2008).

2. An important and highly recommended discussion of the development of trade relations in Europe and the Christian roots of the American free-market economy is to be found in: Rodney Stark, *The Victory of Reason: How Christianity Led to Freedom, Capitalism, and Western Success* (New York: Random House, 2005).

3. Mark Raby, "Online Purchases Exceed $100 Billion in 2006," TGDaily.com. January 4, 2007, http://www.tgdaily.com/content/view/30564/ (accessed December 28, 2007).

4. Mark Sanborn, *You Don't Need a Title to Be a Leader* (New York: Currency, 2006).

CHAPTER 11—A RENDEZVOUS WITH DESTINY

1. Ronald W. Reagan, "A Time for Choosing."

2. Nathaniel Philbrick, *Mayflower : A Story of Courage, Community, and War* (New York: Penguin, 2007).

3. Alexis de Tocqueville, *Democracy in America* (Chicago, IL: University of Chicago Press, 2002), 693.

4. QuoteDb.com, "Thomas Jefferson Quotes," http://www.quotedb.com/authors/thomas-jefferson (accessed January 21, 2008).

5. For more on this remarkable address and other speeches and quotations by the British Prime Minister, visit The Churchill Centre online at http://www.winstonchurchill.org/i4a/pages/index.cfm?pageid=388.

Index